IMPATIENT CRUSADER

Florence Kelley's Life Story

 University of Illinois Press, Urbana, 1953

Impatient

Crusader

By Josephine Goldmark

Felix Frankfurter

Foreword

The pages that follow give an account of the life of a woman who had probably the largest single share in shaping the social history of the United States during the first thirty years of this century. Any such limitation of time regarding influence of a vital force like Florence Kelley is artificial. During that period hers was no doubt a powerful if not decisive role in securing legislation for the removal of the most glaring abuses of our hectic industrialization following the Civil War. But we owe her an even deeper and more enduring debt for the continuing process she so largely helped to initiate, by which social legislation is promoted and eventually gets on the statute books.

The domestic problems of our country after the Reconstruction period may be said to have revolved in the main around the responsibilities of wealth to commonwealth. Those were the problems that were Mrs. Kelley's concern, and for her "wealth" was not shorthand for "plutocrats." It merely implied the utilization of the labor of others for profit. Fly-by-night subcontracting in tenement houses created situations as disregardful of human dignity and as responsible for stunted childhood as were the mighty steel mills or enormous textile factories. And in her view it was equally true that enterprise, both petty and gigantic, may, if unchecked by legislation, deny children the rights of childhood and exploit the economic needs of women—not because of man's inhumanity to man but because they "know not what they do."

There are two kinds of reformers whose chief concern has been that earning a living shall not contradict living a life. One type is apt to see evil men behind evils and seeks to rout evil by moral fervor. Florence Kelley belonged to the other, the cooler and more calculating type. Not that she was without passion. But passion was the driving force of her mind, not its substitute. She early realized that damning facts are more powerful in the long run than flaming rhetoric, and that understanding is a more dependable, because more permanent, ally than the indignation of the moment. No painstaking natural scientist in his laboratory worked more faithfully to verify an experiment than did Mrs. Kelley in digging out and assaying the much more elusive, the far less verifiable data of the sociologist. By the toilsome and heartbreaking exploration of the actual conditions in industry, particularly in so far as they affected the employment of children and women, Mrs. Kelley discovered the truth, and by her indefatigable pen and eloquent tongue gave the truth.

She was like a general in making the truth prevail over the forces of darkness—the darkness not of evil but of ignorance. She went about winning cohorts, men and women whose consciences she could ignite, and whose minds she could educate to serve as constructive guides to their consciences. She realized that a few people who cared, and who knew why they cared, would serve as infectious forces in influencing their environment. So commonplace has telling social investigation become in our day, such progress has been made in securing a quantitative basis for removing social abuses, that it is hard to realize how much we owe to the pioneer efforts of Florence Kelley and the co-workers whom she won to her causes. It is not the function of these few introductory words to summarize the exciting story of Florence Kelley's undaunted efforts to eliminate what she helped to reveal as the ugly concomitants of our stupendous industrial development—child labor, unconscionable hours of work, particularly for women, exploitingly low wages, a shockingly high rate of infant and maternal mortality, neglect of safeguards against occupational diseases. I may, however, give assurance that it is an exciting story.

Without haste and without rest this great general enlisted for the duration of her life to prevent the economic forces of society that were designed for the well-being of man from making inroads upon his well-being. Possessed of a deep understanding of the processes of government, she saw that it is not enough to deal with evils to which modern industry gives rise by episodic crusades. From the beginning of her work as a chief inspector of factories for Illinois she realized the importance of effective administration and all that it implies—a system of alert oversight, a permanent, trained non-political inspectorate, reliable statistics, illuminating reports as the basis of continuous public education. And as she went from Chicago to New York and from New York everywhere throughout the United States, with the National Consumers League and its local affiliates as the instruments of her inspiring leadership, she translated her ardent democratic faith into practical terms and definite, realizable aims. She based her efforts for legislative reforms on wide popular support, the support of a public educated to be responsive to its responsibility, and asserting it not with the ardor of rhetoric but with the impact of hard fact.

It was the same combination of scientist and humanitarian in Florence Kelley that gave her victory in 1912, after six years of effort in partnership with another notable woman, Lillian D. Wald, in seeking the establishment of the United States Children's Bureau. Today it is difficult to understand the resistance to the establishment of this scientific bureau that was to do for ameliorating knowledge regarding child life in the United States what the Department of Agriculture had long ago done for knowledge about pigs. Today when the Children's Bureau is as much taken for granted as is the Bureau of Animal Industry, one can hardly recall, except as something very funny, the attacks that were made on the early publications of the Bureau which proved our high infant mortality rate as compared with that of other countries, and particularly on the disclosure of the vast disparity in the death rates among infants in different sections of the same cities.

It is good that all this should seem like a foolish or weird dream of the past, but it is not good that similar absurd and destructive attacks should be made against equally wholesome measures in our day.

This book ought to be read by all who are immediately concerned with problems of government and by all whose duty it is to enlighten the public. Florence Kelley's life imparts a sense of perspective, it helps us to realize that the familiar is not the necessary. The story also fills one with hope. Florence Kelley spoke of herself as "the most unwearied hoper" in the United States. Newton Baker said of her, "Everybody was brave from the moment she came into a room." Her courage is contagious even from the printed page. The story of her life also carries two indispensable lessons for a democratic society, humility and tolerance: humility in not assuming that our own narrow views, however much we may cherish them, represent eternal truth rather than beliefs derived from a limited experience; tolerance toward differing views of fellow Americans whose motives may be no less pure than our own and whose aim may be the national welfare no less than ours.

To write as lifelessly as I have written about Florence Kelley is to write about her as though she had been merely an institution. The least self-regarding of people, she dedicated her life to the well-being of others. Yet such is the power of personality that she remains in the memory of all whose lives she crossed as one of the most vivid of experiences. She was an inextinguishable flame. From time to time, at different periods, nature in her mysterious ways concentrates in producing a group of remarkable people. Florence Kelley was one of a galaxy of wonderful women with whom she worked—Jane Addams, Julia Lathrop, Lillian D. Wald, Grace and Edith Abbott, Alice Hamilton, among others. Florence Kelley seemed at the time, and remains in memory, the most salient, salty character of them all.

This book is the life of an extraordinary woman by a remarkable woman. In her own exquisite way Josephine Goldmark, a younger co-worker of Florence Kelley, belonged to the galaxy I have mentioned. I wish I could express in more adequate words my feelings of gratitude to Florence Kelley and Josephine Goldmark for the examples they afford of high purposes pursued with gaiety not unmixed with passion, pursued with consecrated devotion not tainted by self-righteousness.

January, 1953
Washington, D.C.

Elizabeth Brandeis

Preface

It has been my privilege to complete the final revision of this book. My aunt, Josephine Goldmark, was well along in revising her manuscript at the time of her death in December, 1950.

Josephine Goldmark was pre-eminently qualified to write about Florence Kelley and her work as a chapter in American social history. For the greater part of Mrs. Kelley's career as general secretary of the National Consumers League, Josephine was her close associate, friend, and fellow worker. Her official title, publications secretary, does not adequately convey the breadth of her contribution to the Consumers League. I am sorry that with her characteristic modesty and reticence she tells in this book so little about herself and her own share in the work. I hope the reader will come to realize from a few remarks scattered here and there in these pages something of the influence she exerted and the way in which she and Mrs. Kelley worked together through the years, so that Consumers League thinking, policy, and achievement were quite largely a joint product.

Josephine Goldmark's feeling about Mrs. Kelley is summed up in the Preface of one of her books: "To Mrs. Kelley I owe gratitude for years of the most generous association in the work of the National Consumers League and for the stimulus of that pure spirit of justice towards all mankind of which she is, as it were, a voice and an embodiment."

Contents

Chapter 1

Home and Heritage

When Florence Kelley was twelve years old, her father took her to see a great steel plant. It was in 1871, and the manufacture of steel by the new Bessemer process promised, her father explained, a rich and magnificent future for America.

They made the journey at night, and the molten metal seemed fierce and alive as it poured from the great furnaces. But it was not this gigantic spectacle in the glare of the furnaces that made the chief impression on Florence that night. It was the sight of little boys, younger than herself, working in the midst of this terrifying scene, carrying pails of water from which the men around the furnaces eagerly drank.

Florence never forgot the boys seen in this dramatic setting, nor other small boys whom she saw at work that same summer in another great industrial enterprise to which her father took her. This was a glass factory. Again there was the excitement of a night journey, the terrific heat of furnaces, figures black against the red glow. In front of the blower's oven stood the glass blower with his long blowpipe and at his feet crouched one of the blower's "dogs," as the young boys were called, who fetched and carried.

"There was a picture I carried with me all my days,"

Florence Kelley wrote long afterwards. She was to recall these first vivid impressions when, as Chief Inspector of Factories for Illinois, she inspected glass houses twenty-odd years later and found similar scenes still being enacted.

I first met Mrs. Kelley at the turn of the century when she was forty years old. She was then general secretary of the National Consumers League, and my sister Pauline had become secretary of the New York City branch. When I joined them in their little office at the corner of Twenty-second Street and Fourth Avenue, I worked at first as a volunteer, doing odd jobs. That was the beginning for my sister and me of a long association with the most exhilarating and generous of companions.

Today Florence Kelley is vaguely known as one of a group of remarkable women who made their mark in fields of general welfare during the first third of the century—Jane Addams, Julia Lathrop, Lillian Wald, and others. But few are aware that Mrs. Kelley was a seminal force in American life. She was, indeed, unique. For over thirty years she traveled the length and breadth of the country, the bearer of a message, the passionate advocate of a cause: the cause of justice. She told at first hand, with eloquence and fire, the story of human exploitation in American industry, primarily of working children and women, of unorganized workers in general.

At the turn of the century and for years afterward, the twelve-hour day and seven-day week still prevailed in steel and many other industries. The sweatshop was rampant. In many states women and young girls worked long hours unregulated by law. Child labor was general, beginning at ten or twelve years. Except to a few specialists, such terms as "minimum wage," "industrial disease," and "maternal mortality" were unknown.

Florence Kelley was well equipped to present the facts of the case against industry. Her voice was heard, and her influence was dynamic among people of the most diverse kinds: in legislatures, schools and colleges, women's clubs, trade unions, churches, and government offices, high and low. No gathering was ever too large, too hostile, or too small and seemingly insignificant for her to address.

It was natural for her to be a leader and, as such, she was soon recognized. Her most distinctive contribution, in the early years, was her insistence on something today accepted as basic, but then a more or less novel idea—her insistence on prevention of social ills. What lay *behind* poverty and misery among wage earners? What caused the sickness, the broken homes, the employment of young children? To these basic questions Mrs. Kelley sought from the outset to direct public attention. "Why," she asked, "do we *have* widows?" It was primarily the high death rate among men workers which caused widowhood and child labor. The evils of industrial life were then largely unrealized or ignored: the work accidents and diseases which annually killed thousands of fathers; the preventable maternal mortality which each year destroyed thousands of homes; the hazards to health from over-fatigue, due to excessive or too intensive hours of work; substandard wages prolific of countless ills. In the movement to study and to prevent these social and industrial evils, Florence Kelley was a pioneer.

Florence Kelley inspired a devoted following. She also made enemies; no one so forthright, so uncompromising, as she was in many respects, could avoid bitter opposition. Those who heard her indictment of our industrial society sometimes felt that she over-dramatized its evils. But mostly they had to accept her basic thesis: first, that the evils were very real, and second, that being man-made they were not inevitable; they could be remedied if the public felt sufficiently responsible. To evoke that sense of social responsibility was Florence Kelley's special gift. She was unequaled in her ability to arouse moral fervor—the mainspring of the hard, determined effort needed to achieve remedial measures.

Thus the story of her life is inevitably bound up with the movements in which she exerted so basic an influence. For all the breadth of her interests, she canalized her efforts in one particular stream, the protection of childhood and the defense of girls and women and unorganized workers in industry. The story of her life explains how this happened.

Florence Kelley was born in 1859, of a cultivated and well-to-do family. Unlike the two contemporaries and life-long friends with whom she began her professional career, Jane Addams and Julia Lathrop, both midwesterners, Florence Kelley was born within four miles of Independence Hall in Philadelphia.

In the few delightful chapters of her autobiography which Paul Kellogg persuaded her to write in 1926 (never, alas, completed), Mrs. Kelley has left a significant record, as she saw it, of her early setting—the impress of heredity and environment upon a sensitive child.[1] She describes her roots in American history, the part played by her family in the great past of the nation, in peace and war alike. The loving detail about her family may serve as a measure of the emotion, rarely expressed, which she felt in face of the per-secution she suffered during the twenties, when attacks upon her as the leader in "radical legislation" filled pages of the *Congressional Record*. She was called the arch-conspirator of the Bolsheviki, determined to obtain legislation "national-izing" American children. On July 8, 1926, for instance, Sen-ator Bayard of Delaware read into the *Record* thirty-five pages of such charges against her and the other defenders of the Children's Bureau, the child labor amendment, and similar legislation. Such attacks might be ignored, but at the cost of a resentment no less deep because suppressed. Florence Kelley's whole life refuted charges so fantastic.

[1] *Survey Graphic*, October 1, 1926, p. 3; February 1, 1927, p. 557; April 1, 1927, p. 31; June 1, 1927, p. 271.

But when at last she wrote something of herself and her background, the suppressed emotion found utterance.

Her ancestry on both sides was varied, typically American in its mingling of diverse strains—Irish, English, and Huguenot. And typically American, also, were the family traditions handed down and never forgotten by the eager child in whose memory they were stored—stories of migration to America on the part of her forebears to escape oppression and to find freedom of worship; of their service in the wars of the colonies and of the states and in the opening of a continent; of Quaker steadfastness and love of peace.

Throughout her young years, Florence's father was the dominant influence in her life. She loved him with a deep devotion, and in his study, from which she "was never willingly absent when he was at home," and in long walks together, she enjoyed the close association with him which she cherished in memory. Through him, history, past and present, became reality for her. She absorbed it at first hand.

William Darrah Kelley, Florence's father, was for almost thirty years a member of the United States House of Representatives. He was the son of a line of Protestant Kelleys from Londonderry, Ireland, and perhaps it was from these Irish forebears that Florence got her quick wit, her fun, and her fighting spirit. Her father's earliest known ancestor had come over from the north of Ireland and settled in New Jersey in 1662.

Florence's father went to work at the age of eleven as errand boy in a printing house, working often from early morning to dark. To this early strain he attributed the nervous excitability which distressed him throughout his life. After a boyhood of hard work, he managed to read law and to gain admittance to the bar of Pennsylvania, and thereafter made his mark.

He was for nine years (1847-56) a judge in Philadelphia. In 1856 he ran for Congress with Frémont on the Free Soil ticket. In 1860 he was a delegate to the Wigwam Convention at Chicago which nominated Lincoln, and was himself elected to the House, to which he was re-elected fourteen times. He was a member of the Ways and Means Committee which in 1869 went to Utah to see the famous "Golden Spike" driven home, uniting the eastern and western halves of the first transcontinental railroad. From that journey he brought back a delightfully illustrated volume called *The Resources of California*. On Florence's tenth birthday, in 1869, her father found her sitting on the floor of his study absorbed in this volume, and from that time on he shared with her whatever she could understand of his activities.

In Congress he was known as Pig-Iron Kelley, the determined champion and fighter for a high tariff for basic American industries. His daughter was to develop convictions diametrically opposed to his; there were to be between them differences of opinion and even, for a time, estrangement. But looking back from the vantage ground of her sixty years, she ascribes to him the first kindling of her ardor for a "juster, nobler, happier life for all American people once a firm industrial foundation, as he saw it, had been laid."

"I wish I had time and strength to send you a full description of my father's companionship to which he admitted me when I was ten years old," she wrote a correspondent in 1926. "Throughout the six years until I entered Cornell in 1876, he talked with me at great length at our home in Philadelphia and wrote me frequently letters adapted to my age and interest during the sessions of Congress.

"To his influence throughout those six years of my early girlhood, I owe everything that I have ever been able to learn to do."

Besides this dominant influence, Florence's youth was affected also by a totally different heredity and environment—that of her Quaker forebears, and the Quaker home in which much of her childhood was spent. Her mother was Caroline Bartram Bonsall, a direct descendant of the famous

Quaker botanist, John Bartram. Caroline Bartram Bonsall's parents died in her childhood. She was adopted by Isaac and Elizabeth Kay Pugh who had been close friends of her parents. It was in their peaceful Quaker home in Germantown that Caroline Bonsall grew up, and with these Pugh "Grandparents," as Florence always called them, she spent some of the happiest years of her childhood.

An important figure in the Pugh background, of whom Florence heard many stories, was the famous chemist and Unitarian minister, Joseph Priestley, who was bitterly persecuted in England because of his non-conformist religion and his sympathy with the ideas of the French Revolution. In 1791 his Unitarian chapel in Birmingham was burned and his house and laboratory sacked by the mob, the labor of years in chemical research destroyed. In 1794 he decided to emigrate to America; with him sailed a family named Kay who had long been his friends and supporters. Elizabeth Kay, whom Isaac Pugh married, was a daughter of these Kays, and the name of Joseph Priestley was revered in the Pugh family.

Besides her adopted Grandmother and Grandfather Pugh, a third figure in the household was to leave a mark upon young Florence Kelley. This was Great-Aunt Sarah Pugh, her grandfather's sister, one of those silent little Quakeresses who devoted themselves wholly to great causes. She was an eager abolitionist, an advocate of woman suffrage, free trade, peace, and the single standard of morals for men and women, sitting, as young Florence noted, "at least half of every day at her desk in her room, writing to Cobden and Bright, to John Stuart Mill, Lady Stanley of Alderley, and the Duchess of Sutherland, and later for many years to Mrs. Josephine Butler, of sainted memory, throughout her terribly painful crusade to abolish the Contagious Diseases Act in England." Even this cause, Great-Aunt Sarah thought proper to share with fifteen-year-old Florence. The latter's lifelong devotion to the relief of oppressed women thus had its roots deep in her past.

A whole new world opened before her when she first realized that Great-Aunt Sarah never used sugar, even in her tea, and wore linen instead of cotton underwear.

"Aunt Sarah, why does thee never eat sugar?" she asked, as she watched her Great-Aunt skillfully mending the fine linen while telling of her English correspondents.

"Cotton was grown by slaves, and sugar also," Great-Aunt Sarah replied. "So I decided many years ago never to use either and to bring these facts to the attention of my friends."

This personal refusal to condone or participate in slave labor by using its product impressed Florence deeply. Many years later she remembered Great-Aunt Sarah's practical philosophy when she laid similar stress upon the individual responsibility of us *all* for the conditions under which the goods we use are made.

In 1850, Caroline Bonsall, the adopted daughter of Isaac and Elizabeth Pugh, married William Darrah Kelley. Her daughter writes of her with deep compassion. She had eight children, all of them fine, healthy babies; yet five of them died in infancy and early childhood.

All this grief, this anguish of frustrated hope [Florence Kelley wrote many years later], occurred, not on the plains as a hardship of pioneer life, not in the Great American Desert where physicians were out of reach, but within four miles of Independence Hall, in one of the great and famous cities of the Nineteenth Century. These tenderly cherished young lives were sacrificed not to the will of God, as mothers were taught throughout the long history of the race, but as we know now, to the prevailing ignorance of the hygiene of infancy . . . from infections now universally recognized as preventable and actually prevented more effectually every year.[2]

When Congress refused, in 1925, to continue appropriations for the law which had for four years provided federal

---

[2] *Survey Graphic,* October 1, 1926, p. 50.

infant and maternity aid to the states, Mrs. Kelley's invective against this action seemed to some too violent. Her question, "Why does Congress wish babies to die?" seemed theatrical. But her plea for this new national policy, her reiteration of the terrible statistics of infant and maternal mortality, was not meant to be an objective argument. Filled with the tragedy of her mother's grief, she spoke in the passionate accents of bereavement, for all stricken mothers.

Florence's father, like Great-Aunt Sarah, believed that even young children should know about boys and girls less fortunate than themselves. He taught her to read when she was seven years old, from a "terrible little book" with woodcuts of children at work in English brickyards, balancing heavy loads of wet clay on their heads. And so Florence began very early in life to hate the sight of little children hard at work.

Her school life was often interrupted, because she was highly susceptible to infection, and her mother feared the possible loss of her last surviving daughter. Of her various short periods of school attendance, always abruptly terminated by some illness, she remembered best the Friends School at Fifteenth and Race streets, in Philadelphia, and the Fourth Day meetings in the quiet of the Friends Meeting House.

In the absence of regular schooling, she found in her father's library something of a substitute. She read it through between her tenth and seventeenth years, beginning with the books near the ceiling and working down toward the floor. She read Shakespeare, Milton, Byron, Goldsmith, and Scott in nine volumes. There were long shelves of history, including the works of Madison, Webster, Bancroft, Prescott, and Francis Parkman.

"Fortunately for me," she said later, "Emerson, Channing, Burke, Carlyle, Godwin, and Spencer were near the floor. I was nearly fifteen when I arrived at them."

One winter, when she lived in Washington, D.C., she

read voraciously in the Library of Congress. "Only the circumstance that I was a very lonely child deeply ashamed of having no school experience, and was thereby goaded to strive against my consequent ignorance by my own unguided effort, could have kept me at work six years (nearly seven) upon this huge, indigestible, intellectual meal." [3]

When Florence's early formative years came to an end, she was mature in many respects beyond her age, and had become awakened to many of the realities of the world about her. In her unfinished autobiography she sums up those early years in one felicitous paragraph:

In Father's library, in the tranquil home at Germantown, in the conscience-searching Fellowship of the Friends, I had divined depths and breadths of human experience in the universe lying beyond our sheltered household life. My Father's boyhood struggle, my mother's tragic loss of five little children, the serene front of my grandparents toward the misfortunes of middle life gave me, as a cherished child, inklings of hazards in the lives of my less fortunate contemporaries. There was Aunt Sarah's conviction that deep rooted evils could be eradicated only by stirring the minds of the oncoming generation; there was Father's charge to prepare for great tasks awaiting his children. And moving through a child's imagination were Free Soilers and Revolutionary ancestors, Quakers and Abolitionists and Non-Conformists, family figures who had put their consciences to the test both of endurance and action. Such were the homes and heritage of one Philadelphia child. . . .[4]

[3] *Survey Graphic,* October 1, 1926, p. 52.
[4] *Survey Graphic,* October 1, 1926, p. 57.

Chapter **2**

Intellectual Ferment

When Florence Kelley entered Cornell University at the age of sixteen, the school was one of the few in America offering an education to women the equal of that offered to men. It was a new land-grant university, founded in 1865 through Ezra Cornell's endowment and the provisions of the federal Morrill Act which Florence's father had helped to pass.

"Entering college," Florence said, "was for me almost a sacramental experience." The girls were a serious-minded group, conscious of being pioneers. They needed no student government, nor any other. Indeed, in a period which we think of as dominated by Victorian standards, the freedom allowed these early students seems astonishing. There were about seventy girls living in Sage College, a dormitory which had been generously designed for a larger number. The girls were therefore encouraged to invite some of the men students to share their half-empty dining room. From this companionship there followed many friendships and marriages. "Little did we care that there was no music, no theatre, almost no library; that the stairs to the lecture halls were wooden, and the classrooms heated with coal stoves. No one, so far as I know, read a daily paper, or subscribed for a monthly or a quarterly. Our current gossip was Froude's life of Carlyle. We read only bound volumes." [1]

Florence was surprised at the lack of interest in politics. None of her friends wanted to listen to her father's letters from New Orleans, where he was a member of a Congressional committee which "counted in" Hayes as President.

She was deeply impressed when she was invited to join a group reading Swinburne with one of the seniors, M. Carey Thomas, later to be dean and president of Bryn Mawr. What Carey Thomas thought of her is indicated in a letter she wrote later, in April, 1883, to her mother: "Miss Kelley dined with me yesterday and I had a charming talk. . . . She amounts to more than any of the Cornell men and girls, except my artist, Miss Clements. Her legal thesis at Cornell was passed very highly."

The thesis of which Miss Thomas wrote was Florence's study of common and statute law dealing with children. It was written mostly in Washington, D.C., for a severe illness had kept her away from school for a time; she spent the winter of 1881-82 reading and writing in the Library of Congress, and did not receive her degree until 1882. In preparing the thesis she not only read the authorities on the legal status of children, but broadened her background by a study of the few American state labor reports then existing, and the more ample British Factory Inspectors' Reports.

She later described the thesis as "slight," but it accomplished something beyond the college requirements. The choice of subject was a natural one after her father's years of effort to enlist her permanently in behalf of less fortunate children. The writing of the thesis completely turned her sympathies in that direction.

Moreover, she was further being initiated into the cause of women, as well as children. From the beginning of the movement for woman suffrage at the Seneca Falls Convention in 1848, her father and Great-Aunt Sarah had been

[1] *Survey Graphic*, February 1, 1927, p. 559.

staunch supporters. Judge Kelley was an early and frequent speaker for the cause, and became sponsor of the suffrage amendment in the House. After Susan B. Anthony established the custom of holding suffrage conventions in Washington during every Congress, Judge Kelley was relied upon as a regular speaker. Thus young Florence, at an early and impressionable age, was living in the center of the arena. Votes for women became for her a prime objective which would tangibly affect the status of women in all fields—industrial, social, and intellectual.

After graduating from Cornell she learned at first hand the restrictions upon higher education for women. She had decided to study law, and in order to prepare herself further for the legal course she applied to the University of Pennsylvania for permission to enter its graduate school. After much delay, the permission was refused. In the first flush of her eager ambition for knowledge, this early rebuff cut deep. She threw herself into other activities, but the denial to her of opportunities she saw being enjoyed by the young men with whom she had been accepted on terms of equality and friendship at Cornell aroused a resentment which burned within her.

Frustrated in her desire to attend graduate school, Florence, after receiving her bachelor's degree, turned to that one of her interests which was to be lifelong: she started an evening school for working girls in Philadelphia, in some rooms alloted to her by the New Century Club—a modest beginning and one typical of the period.

In later years, with that combination of qualities characteristic of her—her tolerance for slow advance despite the native impatience of her temperament, and her radical convictions—Florence looked back with satisfaction to those classes for girls which she had conducted in 1882. They were the beginning of the New Century Guild, destined to become a useful center for many thousands of members through the years.

And yet, even at this period when she still saw life and the industrial development of America through her father's eyes, some fugitive echoes from another world reached her, dim and confused, but with a prophetic insistence.

A visitor at their Philadelphia home presented her with some German pamphlets bound in flaming red covers. He was an importer of fine laces who made business trips to Europe. His father had been a friend of Karl Marx, and after the headquarters of the First International were transferred to Hoboken in 1872 to save it from partisan strife between socialists and anarchists, this visitor at the Kelleys had taken a mild interest in the organization. From it he had purchased, partly through curiosity, these red pamphlets designed for underground distribution in Germany, and he presented them to Florence to provoke discussion.

They were as startling to her, she later said, as her discovery had been—years earlier—of the reason Great-Aunt Sarah ate no sugar and wore no cotton.

She had never gone further than reading the pamphlets, however; Hoboken and the First International were a world away from her sedate Philadelphia. And not long after her graduation from Cornell she was sent to Europe by her family, to accompany her older brother who had been ordered abroad because of ill health.

It was during their lonely stay at Avignon, France, that a chance event occurred which changed Florence's life. Carey Thomas stopped overnight. After a year of study at Leipzig where she had been denied a degree, Miss Thomas had gone to the University of Zurich, the first European university to open its doors to women students. She was soon to return to America to begin her career as a foremost champion of higher education for women.

To Florence, lonely and depressed, with her brother ill and temporarily blind, this glowing young scholar came as a visitor from another world. Florence heard for the first time that the University of Zurich was open to young women; and to Zurich Florence determined to go, a step filled with consequences beyond anyone's foretelling.

After this period spent with her brother, she passed a memorable summer with her father. Companionship with him had always been precious to her. Now she spent the summer of 1883 walking and traveling with him in England, and the marks of that trip were lasting. Her memory was always photographic, and upon it were impressed pictures of the English "Black Country" (so-called because coal mining and related industries had so desolated the countryside).

As part of this pilgrimage she and her father visited the cottage nailmakers and chainmakers of the Midland counties. Chainmaking was a home industry, and young Florence was struck to the heart by this first spectacle of a sweated woman worker, hammering chains in a lean-to at the back of her two-room cottage, her tears falling on the anvil as she related to Judge Kelley and his daughter the details of her desperate plight. "There was no limit to the hours of work when the unhappy women had material and the order had to be rushed. The owners kept wages at the lowest conceivable notch by lengthening the lists of workers and pitting them against each other. We were told by one woman after another that the uniform answer of the bringer of the raw material to the complaints of the worker was: 'If you don't want this work, there's plenty as does.'" [2]

Here was foreshadowed, in this first horrifying encounter with homework, Florence's future warfare against the sweatshop in the countless forms in which this ugly system was later to manifest itself in the United States.

In September, 1883, she joined her mother and younger brother and carried out her intention of going to study at the University of Zurich.

Zurich itself delighted her. The city at this time was small and simple, with many steep, winding streets. There was ample music and a small repertory theater. There was

[2] *Survey Graphic,* April 1, 1927, p. 33.

the lovely canton forest, extending down almost to the Poly-
technicum, "and between the endless rows of pines," she
said, "wildflowers such as I had never seen. Here we students walked by the hour, arguing in English, French, or
German."

And what was the subject of these long arguments in the
Zurich forest? Zurich, we must remember, had long been a
place of refuge for social revolutionists fleeing from despotic
governments such as Czarist Russia, Imperial Germany, and
the Austria of the Hapsburgs. Here a young American who
had been denied the opportunity of graduate study at home
was learning at first hand a new gospel. She was walking and
talking with "ardent students from a dozen countries who
had been caught by the new wildfire of socialism." The Socialist press had been driven out of Germany and its headquarters were in Zurich. The leaders of the movement frequently came there, and at the first meeting she attended
she was trembling with such excitement that she grasped
the sides of her chair and held on firmly.

What generous heart could fail to respond to a creed
that seemed to promise a new future? Here was the answer
to those agonizing problems of human suffering and injustice
which had underlain her consciousness—problems symbol-
ized by little boys working in the glare of glass house and
steel mill, thin little girls at the Manayunk cotton mills, all
she had heard from childhood of cruelty to colored races,
and all she had recently seen of the stunted Black Country
workers and the cottage chainmakers. Her old universe
shriveled. A brave new world lay before her, and she felt
that first parting of the ways which was to divide her forever
from her father's economic teachings and beliefs. Tariffs,
protection, capitalism itself stood condemned by its failures.

It was at this time that Florence translated into English
a small German volume by Friedrich Engels [3] entitled *The
Condition of the Working Classes in England in 1844.* Flor-

_____
[3] Collaborator and friend of Karl Marx.

ence's translation, which reads today as vividly as though originally written in English, was first published in London in 1887, and later in New York.

The force of the little book lay mainly in the evidence of the official British reports quoted by Engels, such as the Children's Factory Commission of 1833 and the Factories Inquiry of 1842. Doctors, factory inspectors, poor law and sanitary visitors, all painted a dreadful picture of misery and degeneration following the incredibly long hours of work, starvation wages, and other hardships of men, women, and little children employed in the early factory period. Florence had seen enough of the Black Country in 1883 to horrify her. Translating these earlier accounts of industrial conditions helped now to make her a convinced socialist.

In the midst of this intellectual ferment there came to Florence the profoundest of emotional experiences. She fell deeply in love. That winter she had met a young Polish-Russian physician, Lazare Wishnieweski, and in June, 1884, they were married. The doctor, too, was a socialist. Their common enthusiasm for the new order, their common belief in its practicability, heightened Florence's happiness.

But the marriage entered upon with such confident joy was destined for disaster. In 1886 Florence returned with her husband and son Nicholas to America. For five years they lived in New York, where her two younger children were born, her second son John Bartram and her daughter Margaret. Dr. Wishnieweski had expected to establish a successful medical practice in New York, but this expectation was not fulfilled. Disappointment, friction, and estrangement followed. Mounting debts, which had to be met by borrowing, played a major part in the break-up of the marriage. Florence drank deep the bitter cup of disillusionment. She determined to separate from her husband and seek a divorce on the grounds of non-support; but since such a divorce was not obtainable in New York, she had necessarily to move to another state. So she moved in 1891 to Illinois, and there obtained her divorce—receiving custody of her three children and resuming her maiden name.

Now she stood alone in the world with her children to support. Her father had died in 1889. It was a grievous loss, for however much they might have differed in economic outlook, however great the gap between their respective views of life, they had resumed the close relationship of her early youth, deeply consoling to her in the midst of unhappiness.

Except for the few friends who shared her confidence at her time of need, her marriage was thereafter a sealed chapter. She almost never mentioned it or referred to it. Even in her autobiography, intimately revealing her childhood and early youth, she compressed her experiences with marriage into two brief sentences.

In any true appraisal of her character, however, Florence Kelley's marriage is important. Only once or twice in the course of our long intimacy did she speak to me about it. My friendship with Mrs. Kelley was that of a much younger woman, though it pleased her to ignore the twenty years' difference between us. But once, when I expressed sympathy for the painful struggle of a young friend recently divorced and said I wished the marriage had never been, Mrs. Kelley dissented. The episode, she said, was worth all the cost. Let no one wish to undo what satisfied the deepest of human instincts.

However bitter her own experience, there can be no doubt that without her marriage and her lifelong maternal happiness, Florence Kelley would not have reached her full stature. These things tempered certain tendencies which might have driven her somewhat ruthlessly toward her goal. Her deep-rooted feminism, her passionate championship of the rights of women, her denunciation of wrongs still suffered by them were never in conflict with her fundamental belief in the claims of the family. She was, in the intensity of that belief, what might today be called old-fashioned.

She was against wage earning for mothers of young children. The teachings of anthropology coincided with her own deep-seated convictions that in the family lay the basis of civilized life.

Mrs. Kelley's marriage was important also in providing a plausible pretext, in later years, for attacks upon her private life to discredit her public work. She had married a Polish-Russian physician. She had translated Engels, whose name was linked with that of Marx as an archenemy of capitalism. She was herself an avowed socialist. What further evidence was needed to prove her a dangerous radical? It allegedly followed that measures she advocated, such as infant and maternity aid and the child labor amendment, would bring the overthrow of American institutions and the "nationalization of children." It was charged that she had "led, engineered, and promoted more socialistic legislation than anybody else in America" and that "many of the rank and file members of the feminist organizations Mrs. Kelley gets to endorse her great drives know no more about her real plans and objectives than the shock troops of Von Hindenburg knew the strategy of his drives."

Despite the charge made at a Congressional hearing that Florence Kelley was "the only Communist leader trained by Engels," she was no such thing. She had always sharply repudiated communism. For socialism, though, her hopes and her enthusiasm remained high. Indeed, she was prepared, on returning from Europe with her husband in 1886, to devote to the cause whatever spare time she might have. The headquarters of the official Socialist Labor party was close at hand in Hoboken. As the translator of Engels, she might well have expected recognized standing with that group and to have found an opening for her talents. Instead, she was expelled from the party within a year. Why this action was taken by the doctrinaire group in control is not clear. The foreignness of the German-American leaders in Hoboken is emphasized in Jane Addams' explanation that

Mrs. Kelley was read out of the party because the "Russian and German Impossibilists" suspected her fluent English.

In Zurich, Florence's eager enthusiasm for the new doctrine had not blinded her to certain basic differences between herself and the socialist youth of Europe. She had behind her a free and happy past, an expanding pioneer tradition, sharply in contrast with that of the victims of oppression. But a convinced socialist she was always to remain, even though—expelled from the party—she would have to find her future work outside the socialist fold.

She resumed her study of child labor, her critical faculties sharpened by her work in Zurich and by the impact of the English official investigations and reports marshaled by Engels. In contrast, the publications of our various state bureaus of labor statistics were thin and colorless, and told almost nothing of what was happening to children in industry. In letters to the press, Florence stressed the lack of information in the United States, on this crucial issue of child labor, and called for competent investigation.

How far she succeeded in making herself felt at this early period is shown by the fact that in 1889, though holding no public office, she was invited to read a paper on child labor at the seventh annual convention of chiefs and commissioners of labor statistics. Here she emphasized anew the lack of competent statistics and the probable increase of child labor. She called for simultaneous investigation of child labor in a typical industry, to be made by various states; and she suggested the silk industry particularly, because it employed a large number of children and was concentrated chiefly in five eastern states. A similar joint investigation of the condition of boys in the mines of the midwest and western states, with North Carolina as a typical southern state, might also be valuable, she said.

The answer made by Carroll D. Wright, then U. S. Commissioner of Commerce and Labor, showed respect for the sharp criticisms of this young woman. "I have been much interested," he said, "in the position the distinguished essayist has taken in the public press relative to the work of the bureaus." But all he could say in defense was to reiterate the fact that except for Massachusetts, none of the states was equipped to make the kind of enumerations she recommended. In Massachusetts the bureau was commissioned to make a census once every ten years, but Florence was criticizing the lack of *continuous* investigations.

The next year, Florence published a short article [4] on the inadequacy of protective laws for children. The census of 1880 had shown that a million children under fifteen years of age were employed in the United States. "Startling enough," she wrote, "in a nation in which it is supposed that the children go to school and the adults do the work." There was good reason to believe that everywhere outside of Massachusetts child labor was increasing. What would the next federal census show, and the simultaneous investigations of child labor by a number of state bureaus, if that could be brought about? Meantime, our latest national data were ten years old.

At this time, we must remember, there existed practically no civic or welfare organizations in the United States interested in urging any labor legislation. Only the regular labor organizations, said Mrs. Kelley, were working to abolish child labor through the enactment of factory acts and investigations. For them the undercutting of wages through the employment of children was "a life and death question."

The prime argument against child labor, she wrote, is "the humane objection that it makes childhood an object of exploitation . . . yet it is safe to say that this objection has never been a sufficient dynamic power in this country." If it had, the societies for the prevention of cruelty to children would not have remained passive spectators while children were burned or crushed or otherwise injured or killed by the hazards of industrial employment.

---

[4] "Our Toiling Children," *Our Day*, VI (1890) 33, p. 192.

Mrs. Kelley's constructive interest in the child labor problem was beginning to receive recognition. But what she now needed was a permanent salaried position to support herself and her three young children. Could she achieve this in the field of her major interest? There were not many job openings for women in the early nineties. She does not seem to have considered teaching, the usual choice for young women of her caliber. With her background it was natural for her to think of work in the field of charity; and paid workers already were being employed by various agencies. She turned first to Frances Willard's organization, the Women's Christian Temperance Union, but it had nothing to offer her.

At this time, a new movement was evolving in the United States. The first two social "settlements" were founded, independently of one another, in 1889. Hull House was founded by Jane Addams in Chicago, and in New York the College Settlement was set up by a small group among whom Vida Scudder[5] was prominent. Both new undertakings were based on the first English social settlement, Toynbee Hall, founded in 1884. Jane Addams and Vida Scudder had each, at different times, visited Toynbee Hall.

Florence Kelley first went to the College Settlement during her early years in New York to visit a friend. She looked about her with skepticism. "I shall never forget that first introduction—the squalid footlessness of it, as it seemed to me, the heavy air, the noise," she wrote in her notes. Once, in a moment of exasperation, her caustic wit burst forth. They were hiding their lights, these intelligent people, "under a bushel of little boys." But gradually she saw the possibilities of the movement with all manner of civic and industrial as well as individual opportunities opening up on every side. She heard of Jane Addams and of Hull House; and with that

---

[5] The College Settlement Group, according to Vida Scudder, had never heard of Jane Addams until Hull House was actually established.

dynamic courage which was natural to her, she decided to stake everything upon a drastic move. She decided to go to Chicago with her three children and to look for work at Hull House.

Chapter **3**

The Move to Hull House

In the following paragraphs, Florence Kelley describes her first impression of Hull House:

On a snowy morning between Christmas 1891 and New Year's 1892, I arrived at Hull-House, Chicago, a little before breakfast time, and found there Henry Standing Bear, a Kickapoo Indian, waiting for the front door to be opened. It was Miss Addams who opened it, holding on her left arm a singularly unattractive, fat, pudgy baby belonging to the cook who was behindhand with breakfast. Miss Addams was a little hindered in her movements by a super-energetic kindergarten child, left by its mother while she went to a sweat-shop for a bundle of cloaks to be finished.

We were welcomed as though we had been invited. We stayed, Henry Standing Bear as helper to the engineer several months, when he returned to his tribe; and I as a resident seven happy, active years until May 1, 1899, when I returned to New York City to enter upon the work in which I have since been engaged as secretary of the National Consumers' League.

I cannot remember ever again seeing Miss Addams holding a baby, but that first picture of her gently keeping the little Italian girl back from charging out into the snow, closing the door against the blast of wintry wind off Lake Michigan, and tranquilly welcoming these newcomers, is as clear today as it was at that moment.[1]

---

[1] *Survey Graphic,* June 1, 1927, p. 271.

Florence was fortunate in coming to Hull House at this time. She found there the pioneering enthusiasm for a new movement. Jane Addams, after a girlhood spent in study and travel and soul-searching, and some years of semi-invalidism, had discovered for herself—and was offering to others—a new outlet, a new release of energies. Her visit to Toynbee Hall and her study of the English social settlement idea confirmed her belief that here was a way of life in which to help repair the injustices of society.

At this time in the United States, firsthand knowledge of "how the other half lives" was practically non-existent. Jacob Riis's book of that name, the first of a long series which have uncovered the dark places of life, was not published until 1891, two years after Hull House was founded. I remember the excitement with which we undergraduates at Bryn Mawr in the middle nineties listened to Walter Wyckoff, a robust Princeton graduate who had broken new ground by going out in search of a job as an unskilled laborer. A hopeless search he had found it in that depression era.

Jane Addams offered to young people of the awakening middle class in America a new kind of pioneering, an excursion into the unknown, appealing to the generosity, the courage, the restlessness, and the deep desire of youth to make the world over. And because Jane Addams was a woman of great spiritual power, the settlement reflected her own high way of taking life, her conviction that all mortal beings are kin, that whatever degrades any human life degrades us all, and that what elevates it we all share in. The settlement was thus a bridge between the more and the less favored, giving to the former a firsthand acquaintance with the living and working conditions of a newly industrialized society.

Florence Kelley undoubtedly would have agreed with what Alice Hamilton said about Hull House, "To me the life there satisfied every longing—for companionship, for the excitement of new experiences, for constant intellectual stimulation and for the sense of being caught up in a big movement which enlisted my enthusiastic loyalty."[2]

Upon arriving in Chicago, Florence Kelley's first problem was to make arrangements for her children. She did not intend to set up a separate household of her own, nor did she want to have the children live permanently in a great city amid tenement surroundings. She wanted to have them within easy reach, under the right conditions; and by great good fortune she found precisely this combination.

On the day after her arrival in Chicago, Miss Addams took her to the beautiful home of Henry Demarest Lloyd at Winnetka, on Lake Michigan, which for years had been a center of hospitality and intellectual refreshment to many people. There Florence Kelley's three little children spent most of their first winter, alternating with visits to Hull House, "well and happy," she said, "under Mrs. Lloyd's wise, unwearied kindness and exhilarated by unimagined experiences of country freedom and outdoor winter play." Winnetka was within easy reach of Hull House, so that she was in close touch with the children; and there began a friendship with the Lloyds continuing into the third generation.

For Henry D. Lloyd himself, Florence Kelley felt an immense admiration. He was at that time working on his epoch-making book, *Wealth Against Commonwealth,* published in 1894, the fruit of many years' study of monopolies, such as the oil, steel, and coal industries, with their control of the railroads. This was but one of his important contributions to the study of basic economic problems of American life.

Henry Lloyd, like other liberals of the time, had been deeply shaken by a crisis in Chicago in 1886, an event which shook the whole nation: the trial and hanging of the an-

[2] *Exploring the Dangerous Trades* (Boston, 1943), p. 69. Alice Hamilton was another of the early Hull House group, later the outstanding American authority on industrial diseases.

archists in what was known as the "Haymarket bombing."
Hull House was not founded until three years after this
tragic event, but the settlement in general and Florence
Kelley in particular were inevitably swept into the bitter
conflict which long persisted as its aftermath.

During the eighties the world-wide agitation for an
eight-hour day had been carried on in the United States, too.
The unemployed in the country numbered two million, a
small number by later standards but a large one then. The
eight-hour day was sought by the trades unions to reduce
unemployment through spreading work. The dominant labor
group at the time, the Knights of Labor, claiming a million
members, were foremost in the movement. A small anarchist
group, mainly German, who advocated "direct action," or
violent methods to attain their ends, achieved publicity out
of proportion to their numbers or influence. They, too, came
out in favor of the eight-hour day.

May 1, 1886, was set for general strikes and demonstra-
tions throughout the country. In the principal cities many
struck. Thirty thousand gathered in Union Square in New
York, thirty-five thousand in Chicago. A riot occurred near
the McCormick Reaper Works in which the police fired, killing a striker. A mass meeting of protest was called for May 4
in Haymarket Square. And there occurred the tragic events
which cast so black a shadow for decades. A bomb was
thrown, by whom no one knew then or ever after. About
sixty policemen were wounded, and seven were killed.

"The throwing of the bomb killed the eight-hour movement," said Samuel Gompers in later years. But it did far
worse. It precipitated in Chicago and throughout the
country an avalanche of panic. The demand for conviction of
the anarchists who had previously advocated violence was
so intense that eight of the group, one of whom was not
even in Chicago at the time, were arrested and found guilty.
Four were hanged, one committed suicide, and three were
sent to prison.

Six years later, Governor John P. Altgeld pardoned these three for lack of evidence and because of glaring irregularities of procedure in the trial. For this courageous act he was bitterly denounced, not only by the conservative press but by such prominent citizens as Theodore Roosevelt and Lyman Abbott. Indeed, like the Sacco-Vanzetti case many years later in Boston, the Haymarket case almost divided brother from brother. The Hull House group, with Henry D. Lloyd and progressives throughout the country, pressed for the pardon and hence shared in the denunciation poured out upon Governor Altgeld.

Illinois at that period still exhibited what Jane Addams later called "many characteristics of the pioneer country in which untrammelled energy and 'an early start' were the most highly prized generators of success." When the first labor laws were proposed, they "ran counter to the instinct and tradition, almost to the very religon of the manufacturers of the state, who were for the most part, self-made men." Because the Haymarket bombing was associated with the eight-hour movement, it seemed "patriotic" for years to denounce all those connected with a demand for shorter hours and higher wages as "anarchistic" plotters against American institutions. Mrs. Kelley summed up the succession of social conflicts of that era as she saw them in retrospect:

The Haymarket riot, followed in 1888 by the hanging of the Anarchists, the Pullman strike, the great ensuing railroad strike of 1894, with the regular army patrolling the Post Office, and soldiers traveling on mail trains, were treated as they came along, by the press, the public and the government, not as a series of vitally significant occurrences incidental to the sudden, overwhelmingly rapid development of capitalism in this vast rural area; they were treated as disagreeable episodes to be ended somehow and forgotten as quickly as possible.[3]

It is against this sequence of events that we must view Florence Kelley and her associates at Hull House, setting

[3] *Survey Graphic*, June 1, 1927, p. 273.

out to right as best they could some of the immediate social maladjustments among which they were living. Of the group she joined in 1891, Florence Kelley felt closely drawn first of all to Jane Addams, and second to Julia Lathrop. Her early environment and her life up to this time had been different from theirs. Yet she had in common with these two children of Illinois pioneers certain basic experiences which formed a special bond between them.

From their fathers, each of the three had derived a high tradition of public service. Thus, Florence Kelley took pride in her father's career in Congress and especially his part in all that concerned Lincoln. Jane Addams' father and Julia Lathrop's father had both served in the Illinois State Legislature, as Lincoln himself did, during the critical years just before the Civil War. In Springfield, Illinois, as in Washington, D.C., the issues of peace and war hung in the balance.

Thus, the children of abolitionist families in the midwest, like the child of Quaker tradition in Philadelphia and of a radical reconstructionist father, grew up catching the enthusiasm of their elders for the great political issues of their times, and they valued this common background. The similarity of experience of the three friends in the support each received from her father in the women's rights movement also had an important bearing on their development.

When these three were young, the emancipation and the higher education of women were and had been for decades burning issues. When Florence, Jane, and Julia were growing up in the seventies and eighties, the echoes of the early nineteenth-century struggle for women's rights were still reverberating, and the intensity of the early conflict was still poignantly felt.

The women who first spoke out publicly in the early abolitionist movement had been frowned upon as "unsexed," preached against as Jezebels, mobbed, ridiculed, and ostracized. The Grimke sisters, Lucy Stone, Abby Kelly, Lucretia

Mott, Elizabeth Cady Stanton, the Blackwell sisters are a few of the names on that early roll of honor.[4] Susan B. Anthony joined the group somewhat later. The opposition of most men to women's rights aroused intense bitterness, indeed a kind of sex antagonism, tingeing the whole texture of their emotional lives.

The struggle for higher education was one phase of this long warfare. Emma Willard had opened her famous Female Seminary in Troy in 1821; and Oberlin was founded in 1833, and several years later was the first college in the United States to adopt co-education. But the right of girls to a college education was fought for decades, and no part of the battle for women's rights was filled with more bitterness. Thus, as late as the eighties, a leader like Carey Thomas underwent a humiliating struggle before her father would give her the college education her brothers received as a matter of course.

But the three young women of our story were encouraged by their fathers in their educational ambitions, Florence going to Cornell, Julia to Vassar, and Jane to Rockford Academy and later abroad. They knew their fathers stood foursquare for the emancipation of women. Judge Kelley consistently supported equal suffrage. Julia Lathrop's father drafted the bill enabling women in Illinois to be admitted to the bar, and the first woman lawyer in the state read law in his office. Instead of having to combat masculine opposition such as that which inflicted so deep a trauma upon some of their contemporaries, these three more fortunate

---

[4] Younger generations have often assumed that the early women's rights struggle arose from the frustrations of embittered spinsters. On the contrary, many of these pioneers were happily married and were aided in their fight for women's rights by their own husbands. Elizabeth Stanton and Lucretia Mott issued their call for the first famous Seneca Falls Convention of 1848 because they had been excluded from the Great London Abolitionist Meeting of 1842, though sent as delegates from the United States. With them in the gallery sat William Lloyd Garrison, refusing to take part in the meeting in protest against the exclusion of the two women.

young women each had an inner security. Each knew that she had in her father an ally, a steadfast defender of her sex. This sense of security stood them in good stead in their lifelong participation in the struggle for equal justice for women in many fields. Their feminism was no single strand of their being. It was an integral part of their total concern for the weak as against the strong; for children, first of all; for girls and women unable to get their own rights; for exploited workers and the underprivileged in general; and for minorities. Feminism was none the less intense for this inclusiveness. Rather, it gained through the ardor of their emotional response to all human need.

Florence's European experience had led her further in social theory than the two friends to whom she felt so closely bound. Neither Jane Addams nor Julia Lathrop could accept the socialist creed or believe in a fixed class consciousness which they saw contradicted by the fluid conditions of American society. Florence Kelley, socialist though she was, could make common cause with her friends in pursuit of social aims which she shared, even though she thought those aims inadequate.

These were Florence Kelley's closest friends and associates at Hull House. And it was with them that she found, or rather devised for herself, the special training she needed for her later work. This is an aspect of the early days in the settlements which has never received due notice. Settlements such as Hull House were the first centers of social research. Miss Addams, so little given to claiming originality in ideas or superior intuitions, took legitimate satisfaction in claiming this priorty. "In a sense," she writes, "we were the actual pioneers in field research." The settlements antedated by ten years the establishment of the first foundation for social research.[5]

The ordinary incidents of life in a crowded industrial

---

[5] *The Second Twenty Years at Hull-House* (New York, 1930), p. 405.

area threw into harsh relief the hard realities of the work-
aday world. The injuries of three Hull House club boys from
unguarded machinery which killed one of them the first
winter; the refusal of candy by little girls at Christmas because they worked such long overtime hours in a candy
factory that they could not bear the sight of it; the fate of
Chloe, one of the girls at a Hull House club whose name
seemed to fit her delicate charm, who worked to the point
of exhaustion every night at a nearby factory and who was
decoyed early one morning into a saloon and a disreputable
house. Incidents such as these, many times multiplied, gave
to the residents glimpses of what life was like in the neighborhood. The fatal injury of a Hull House boy from an unguarded machine was especially shocking to the residents.
They had expected his employer to share their horror and
to prevent the recurrence of such a tragedy. Instead,
nothing at all was done, and they learned of the system of
"releases" required from the parents of working children
to free the employer from claims of damage in case of injury. Florence Kelley was to store up her indignation at
this cold-blooded system until the time came for her to take
action against it. Meantime, what was obviously needed was
more systematic, carefully collected information about those
areas with which the settlement residents were most familiar.

Florence Kelley's experiences up to this time had well
prepared her to fit into the pattern of work thus opening
before her. In writing her Cornell thesis she had discovered
and learned how to use the British Factory Inspectors' Reports, the best research material on her subject. Her translation of Engels' book had carried her further into study of
these sources. Her trip through the English Black Country
and the sight of the chainmakers' homes had opened her
eyes to undreamed of living conditions. Socialist teaching
had further impressed upon her heart and mind the hardships and the grievances of the workers' lot. Now at Hull

House she was living in the center of an area brimful of
social significance, still largely unexplored. Back of her lay
her sheltered girlhood; her conversion to a new world of
belief; the emotional crisis of her life and the need of re-
building it. Her "novitiate" as she called it, was over. She
was ready to go to work.

At the start she was assigned to the job of advising girls
who were in search of work. "Now it would be called vocational guidance. Then I was called an Employment Agent,"
she wrote later. Thus she was brought at once into personal
contact with working girls and their problems.

It was also during the first year at Hull House that Florence had her first opportunity to do formal research. Carroll
D. Wright, at that time U. S. Commissioner of Commerce
and Labor, was conducting an inquiry into the slums of great
cities. As we have seen, at the meeting of chiefs of bureaus
of labor statistics in 1889, at which Florence Kelley read a
paper, Commissioner Wright had expressed a high opinion
of her comments and other writings on child labor which
had appeared in the public press. He now appointed her to
cover the slum inquiry in the Chicago area.

Florence threw herself into this first field research with
all the eagerness which might have been expected of her.
Under her guidance, a square mile around Hull House was
canvassed. In this area people of eighteen nationalities were
encountered. The outstanding fact was the universality of
tenement homework surrounding Hull House in every direction, pressing men, women, and children into its service,
from the oldest to the youngest, down to three years of age.
"For children can pull out basting threads, sew on buttons,
paste boxes and labels, strip tobacco, and perform a multitude of simple manipulations as readily as they can learn
the kindergarten occupations," she later wrote.

Such homework was lamentably familiar to Hull House
residents in the homes of the neighborhood, but it was unknown to the general public. Florence suggested to the Illi-

nois Bureau of Labor that it, too, should investigate the
sweating system and was herself engaged to make a report
on it. In 1895, that admirable first fruit of social research
known as *Hull House Maps and Papers* was published, con-
taining among other studies the results of Florence Kelley's
sweatshop investigations.

Enough public interest had been aroused by this time
to induce the Illinois State Legislature to consider the need
of some remedial legislation. As a preliminary it appointed
a joint committee of the House and Senate to make its own
investigation. Here was an opportunity for Florence Kelley
to put her research to practical account. She took the lead
in guiding the legislative committee through tenements and
factories and in preparing a report for the legislature. In the
square mile around Hull House, honeycombed with sweatshops, she showed them sights that few legislators had ever
beheld. They took testimony from all sorts of persons involved—employers, employees, doctors, nurses, and other
witnesses. The results were gratifying. "The subject was a
new one in Chicago," wrote Mrs. Kelley later. "For the press
the sweating system was that winter a sensation. No one was
yet blasé."

As part of its report to the legislature, the legislative committee recommended the first factory law for Illinois. In its
regulation of hours the bill proposed was, indeed, revolutionary. In place of no limitation on the hours of women
employed in factories, it proposed, for the first time in the
United States, an eight-hour day by statute. It prohibited
the employment of children under fourteen years in factories. It proposed initial steps to control tenement sweatshops. It created an Illinois State Factory Inspection Department.

Filled with enthusiasm for this new measure, a group of
Hull House residents, led again by Florence Kelley, joined
the labor unions in a vigorous campaign for its passage.
Every evening for three months they addressed meetings of

social clubs, labor groups, church organizations, and benefit societies until the bill was passed. Miss Addams throws an interesting sidelight on this era:

I well recall that on the Sunday the members of this commission came to dine at Hull House, our hopes ran high, and we believed that at last some of the worst ills under which our neighbors were suffering would be brought to an end. . . .

The eight-hour clause in this first factory law met with much less opposition in the Legislature than was anticipated. . . . During the halcyon months when it was a law, a large and enthusiastic Eight-Hour Club of working women met at Hull House, to read the literature on the subject and in every way to prepare themselves to make public sentiment in favor of the measure which meant so much to them.[6]

After the bill was passed, Governor Altgeld had next to appoint the head of the Factory Inspection Department created under the new law. He offered the appointment to Henry Demarest Lloyd, who refused it and suggested instead the name of Florence Kelley.

---

[6] *Twenty Years at Hull-House* (New York, 1924), pp. 185, 188.

Chapter 4

Mrs. Kelley Enforces the New Law

Florence Kelley was appointed Chief Inspector of Factories for Illinois in July, 1893. With a staff of twelve persons and a total appropriation of fourteen thousand dollars, she proceeded to make a name for herself and her department.

She was the first and, until Governor Alfred E. Smith appointed Frances Perkins in New York thirty-five years later, the only woman to head a state factory inspection department. The vigor and tenacity which had led her so far on her path, her moral fervor, and the training acquired in her social research had fitted her well for this office.

At that time (as, indeed, in too many instances today) the administration of labor laws had been the happy hunting ground of the politician, with labor department appointments distributed as political plums. Mrs. Kelley from the first regarded it as a serious scientific undertaking, the importance of which was unappreciated by the public. In later years she wrote:

A black chapter in our industrial history is this of our treatment of our factory inspectors; they have been left in the position of hostile critics, prosecutors—of corporations infinitely more powerful than themselves. Within the factory they have been met as enemies, bribed when possible, and in shamefully numerous cases, removed from office when they could be neither bribed, tricked, nor intimidated.

Under these sorry conditions the scientific output of these officials is naturally valueless. . . . Neither men nor women can do what needs to be done until our whole attitude toward the task is fundamentally changed.[1]

As we have seen, Mrs. Kelley had early pointed out the inadequacy of the reports of state bureaus of labor. As a layman she had demanded in such reports facts and figures which the "plain man" could understand. Speaking for taxpayers, she had asked for concrete information on which intelligent action could be based. As Newton Baker once said, "Mrs. Kelley paid to human beings the high compliment of believing that, once they knew the truth, they would want to act upon it. Hence her insistence upon the adequate presentation of facts."

As a responsible enforcing official, she now, in 1893, lived up to the standards she had demanded. Her four annual reports as Chief Inspector of Factories were something new in the dusty area of state publications. They are not like other official reports. In the words of two discriminating critics: "So moving and human are they, so full of indignant satire, so honest in their relentless description of conditions as they really existed, with no attempt to cover up or conceal the evils with which the state must deal." [2]

Child labor, sweatshops, accidents, judges remote from industrial life yet with power to mold it, all come to life in these vivid pages.

It is readily understandable that in her new position, Florence Kelley's experience and her own deep maternal instincts predisposed her to give a prominent place to the enforcement of the child labor sections of the new law. The

[1] *Modern Industry in Relation to the Family, Health, Education, and Morality* (New York, 1914), p. 67.

[2] Edith Abbott and Sophonisba P. Breckinridge, *Truancy and Non-Attendance in the Chicago Schools* (Chicago, 1917), p. 75.

conditions she encountered in the Illinois of 1893 were well calculated to emphasize this need.

The only previous law affecting the employment of children was one prohibiting children under fourteen years of age to work in mines. In addition, a city ordinance of Chicago forbade the employment of any child below the age of ten years at any gainful occupation *unless* the child had dependent upon it a decrepit adult relation. Many early child labor laws contained this grotesque proviso, and Florence Kelley was to spend many a year fighting it and pointing out the anomaly of burdening a child with responsibilities which the community would ultimately take over, as a matter of course. Today we realize that the final cost to society, in the form of ill health and juvenile delinquency, of the orphans and other children permitted to work because they are assumed to be the sole supporters of elderly relatives, is much greater than the cost of relief or rehabilitation for the adults involved.

The new law forbade employment of children under fourteen years in factories, or longer than eight hours, or at night, or without an affidavit of age. Since these affidavits were made by parents anxious to put their children to work, they were often not reliable. Indeed, inspectors found hundreds of children whom they had good reason to believe were under fourteen duly provided with affidavits.

Viewed as an "initial measure" the new law was a promising beginning, but Mrs. Kelley never allowed the people of the state to believe that it was anything more than that. Compared with the codes of seven other states,[3] it did not effectively guard the children "in their life, limbs, health, or intelligence." It was "far from insuring the people of the state," she adds caustically, "against an increasing burden of orphan children and of cripples, consumptives, and other

[3] Massachusetts, New York, New Jersey, Pennsylvania, Ohio, Michigan, and Rhode Island. *Second Annual Report of the Factory Inspectors of Illinois,* 1894.

invalids, deprived of the power of self-support by preventable evils in the places in which they work."

For four years Mrs. Kelley kept up a running fire against the failure of the Chicago Board of Education to enforce the Compulsory Education Law. For although the Child Labor Law prohibited the employment of children under fourteen years of age in manufacturing, it could not be adequately enforced unless the children were kept in school. This the Board of Education consistently failed to do.

The Chicago school census of 1894 showed 6,887 children, between the ages of seven and fourteen, out of school. Thousands of these were roaming the streets, peddling, floating from job to job. Yet the Board of Education relied only upon "moral suasion" to get parents to send their children to school. What was needed, insisted Mrs. Kelley, was the prosecution of parents who disobeyed the Compulsory Education Law. Prosecution should be made mandatory upon boards of education just as prosecution of manufacturers was made mandatory upon the factory inspectors. Otherwise the work of her department was largely nullified. One autumn, as a test, she reported to the Board of Education 103 children under fourteen years found at work. Only 31 of these were ever placed in school. She showed the shocking illiteracy among children resulting from such a policy.[4]

Spectacular abuses in child labor were still rampant when Mrs. Kelley took office. Of these the most intolerable were in the stockyards and the glass factories.

The number employed in the stockyards was not large. In her report for 1894 Mrs. Kelley lists 302 boys and 18 girls found at work there. But the conditions of employment then existing aroused her horror. That any human being should be subjected to such scenes and stenches was an outrage; how much more outrageous for young boys in their impressionable years. She had no legal power to stop these

---

[4] Not until almost ten years later, in 1903, was a more adequate compulsory education law passed.

practices, but the public should at least know the truth. She would spare them none of the revolting details.

Some of the children are boys who cut up the animals as soon as the hide is removed, little butchers working directly in the slaughter house, at the most revolting part of the labor performed in the stockyards. These children stand, ankle deep, in water used for flooding the floor for the purpose of carrying off blood and refuse into the drains; they breathe air so sickening that a man not accustomed to it can stay in the place but a few minutes; and their work is the most brutalizing that can be devised.

Other young boys were working in a foul, dark passage at an unguarded machine where the smell of the smoking bones and rags of hide

excels in horror all the smells for which the stockyards are notorious. . . . No criminal in the United States could be punished by an hour's imprisonment in such a place without a horrified protest ringing through the land.

Worst of all, such conditions were unnecessary, preventable.

Nor is there any excuse for the existence of such surroundings. With the facilities for ventilation and deodorizing that are readily available, this passageway could be made inoffensive. Meanwhile the employment of any human beings in such a place is an outrage and should be summarily stopped, but the law confers upon the inspectors no power to stop it.

Mrs. Kelley uncovered abuses equally glaring in the employment of young boys in the glass factories. What she saw in Alton, Illinois, brought back vividly the midnight scene impressed forever on her as a child in Pennsylvania: the sight of the blowers' boys trotting steadily to and fro in the fierce glare of the furnaces.

Here they were in Illinois, running to and fro in just the same fashion. Mrs. Kelley made a special report to Governor Altgeld on the glass industry in Alton. Dickens himself, in his crusades against cruelties to children, might have painted the picture. The factory law was being successfully evaded,

by dissolute men and women who gathered in orphan and deserted children from the poorhouses of five counties adjacent to that in which stands the city of Alton, and from the orphan asylums in St. Louis, and made affidavits as "guardians" of the children that the lads were fourteen years of age when they were really from seven to ten years. The "guardians" then proceeded to live upon the earnings of the children which were, in 1893, forty cents a day for small boys and sixty cents for larger ones.

The earnings of the skilled glass blowers depended somewhat upon the speed of the boys who fetched and carried for them. Hence they, as well as the employers and the press and even the local relief agency in Alton, foretold dire sufferings from enforcement of the new Child Labor Law. The employers threatened to close the factories. None of these prophecies of doom came true, and as in other industries, the removal of the children resulted in time in the installation of mechanical contrivances to replace them.

Mrs. Kelley's accounts of what she had found at Alton remained vivid to those who heard them at first hand. Many years later Alice Hamilton described the glass house boys as Mrs. Kelley had made them live for the Hull House residents: "As she drew the picture we saw these little figures drawn from the orphan asylums and put in flat-boats and drifted down the river to Alton and sent into work as blower dogs, working by night or day, at any age they might be. She had been down there and seen them on the night shift and she had stood outside at the door and had seen the night shift come out, these little fellows trotting behind the men they worked for and going perfectly naturally into a saloon with them for a pick-me-up before they staggered home to go to bed." [5]

[5] Alice Hamilton, speech at a memorial meeting in honor of Florence Kelley held at the Friends Meeting House in New York City, March 16, 1932.

Mrs. Kelley found less spectacular hardships for children in other occupations, such as the department stores with closing hours near to midnight at Christmas, in candy factories with their "rush" seasons of almost unlimited hours, and in the street trades.

The worst danger to children lay in the high incidence of accidents from unguarded machinery. "Killing children by machinery has not yet been made a crime in Illinois," commented Mrs. Kelley in her report for 1895.

The Chief Inspector of Factories had no authority to inspect machinery, much less to prosecute for injuries. She could, however, turn the light of publicity on current practices. Thus, in her report for 1895 she cited four fatal accidents and one probably fatal which had occurred in one week among workmen employed at the Illinois Steel Company. If such were the hazards for men, what were the dangers to boys exposed often to the same risks? In one case, a boy was found operating a machine at which his father had just been severely injured, so as to hold the job for him.

"That the company is fully aware of the danger to children," she wrote, "is shown by its policy of requiring the following release from the parents of minors employed by it":

I . . . parent as aforesaid fully recognize the hazardous nature of the employment in which my said son is about to engage, but nevertheless I, the said parent . . . consent to such employment of said minor, and in consideration thereof . . . I do hereby release and forever discharge the Illinois Steel Co. of and from all claims . . . for loss of service of said minor on account of any personal injuries he may sustain while in the employ of said company.

Similar releases required by the Wabash Railroad Company and the Chicago Drop Forge and Foundry Company were published in the same report.

It is a far cry from such accepted practice to the triple compensation for accidents to illegally employed minors initiated by Wisconsin in 1917, a goal urged by Mrs. Kelley for every state in the Union. Compensation, so-called, for industrial injuries (for what money can compensate physical disability?) had by that time become a part of our accepted national policy. Double or triple compensation for children illegally employed was gradually becoming law. It was Florence Kelley who early insisted upon publication of the facts, as the necessary prerequisite for remedial legislation.

Mrs. Kelley's efforts to enforce the child labor sections of the Illinois law had one unpremeditated result. Her first attempt to impose the penalty for employing children without the prescribed "working papers" led her to the office of the district attorney of Cook County. She laid before him complete evidence for a case. A boy of eleven years, illegally employed at gilding cheap picture frames by means of a poisonous fluid, had lost the use of his right arm. There was at that time no compensation law covering industrial accidents and diseases, and no legal enforcement of safety measures covering work in dangerous trades. The only responsibility of the employer—he had none toward the child employee—was a fine of twenty dollars for employing a child of that age without the required certificate.

The district attorney was a brisk young politician with no interest in the new law or in the special case brought to him. Mrs. Kelley described the interview between them:

The young official looked at me with impudent surprise and said in a tone of astonishment: "Are you calculating on *my* taking the case?"

I said: "I thought you were the district attorney."

"Well," he said, "suppose I am. You bring me this evidence this week against some two-by-six cheap picture-frame maker, and how do I know you won't bring me a suit against Marshall Field next week? Don't count on me. I'm overloaded. I wouldn't reach this case inside of two years, taking it in its order." [6]

Her reaction was characteristic and immediate. That day she registered as a law student at Northwestern Univer-

---

[6] *Survey Graphic,* June 1, 1927, p. 274.

sity. The lectures were given in the evenings and so did not interfere with her regular work. Credit was allowed for the law reading she had done with her father in Washington in 1882 and for her studies in Zurich. In June, 1894, she received her law degree. Although she never practiced law, her legal training was valuable in connection with her future career.

The new Illinois factory law undertook also to provide some measure of control over sweatshop work in the tenements—the widespread evil which had figured so largely in the campaign preceding passage of the act. Owners of goods produced under the sweating system were required to furnish to the factory inspectors complete lists of names and addresses of contractors and homeworkers, and by a drastic requirement, goods found in homes exposed to contagious diseases were required to be destroyed on the spot.

The smallpox epidemic of 1893 in Chicago, following a neglected case on the famous Midway of the World's Fair, threw into high relief the conditions under which garments were made and finished in the tenement sweatshops of Chicago—shockingly overcrowded and totally unsanitary. Efforts were made to hush up the situation. Florence Kelley proceeded to enforce the law.

I knew Florence Kelley at the time of the smallpox epidemic [wrote Judge Andrew Bruce, who had been attorney for the factory inspectors] when both she and Julia Lathrop were risking their lives in the sweatshop district of Chicago and were fearlessly entering the rooms and tenements of the west side and not merely alleviating the sufferings of the sick but preventing the sending abroad of the infected garments to further contaminate the community.

I saw these two women do that which the health department of the great city of Chicago could not do. The authorities were afraid not only of personal contagion but of damage suits if they destroyed the infected garments. They therefore said there was no smallpox in Chicago. Later as the result of a joint attack by Miss

Julia Lathrop and Mrs. Florence Kelley they were induced to act and they destroyed thousands of dollars' worth of clothing.[7]

But after more than three years of effort to follow up contractors and homeworkers, Mrs. Kelley declared these provisions of the law to be non-enforceable. With nearly 15,000 garment workers employed in these shops in Chicago, and the incompleted garments going out to the rooms of home finishers in tenement houses, no staff of inspectors, however large and well equipped, could grapple with the essential evil of tenement house manufacture in great cities.

The 270 garment factories in Chicago she could supervise like other factories, but the little contractors' shops were impossible to control. At one time her staff had counted 2,348 such shops, but some were always failing and opening again in new locations under different names. And it was precisely in these worst places of employment that more and more children were found at work. In other factories and workshops there were 56 children to every 1,000 males over sixteen years; in the sweatshops, 223 children to every 1,000 males over sixteen. For every five men, a little girl under sixteen years of age.

What method of control for homework could be devised? Mrs. Kelley came out boldly for legislation totally prohibiting manufacturers from sending goods to be finished in homes.

Prohibition of tenement homework had been held unconstitutional in New York. It had seemed for years an ultraradical proposal. This system of homework saved the manufacturer the costs of factory rent, light, heat, etc. Just as the myth of the widowed mother relying upon the newsboy's earnings, and the myth of dependent relatives supported by orphans under working age delayed by many years the protection of these children, so the myth of necessity for homework to support families unable otherwise to exist, post-

---

[7] Quoted by Jane Addams in *My Friend, Julia Lathrop* (New York, 1935), p. 118.

poned for two decades any legislation to do away with this form of exploitation. Not until 1913 were the first tentative steps taken in the state of New York to abandon the pretense of regulating this protean monster and to prohibit tenement homework outright.[8]

The most controversial article of the Illinois law of 1893, providing an eight-hour day for women and girls employed in factories, was short-lived. Its constitutionality was soon challenged in the courts, and in 1895 it was declared invalid by the Supreme Court of Illinois. That pronouncement, based on the theoretical "freedom of contract" of workers under the Fourteenth Amendment of the federal Constitution, put an immediate stop to the enforcement of the law on behalf of the 30,000 women and 1,181 young girls found employed that year in Illinois factories and sweatshops, many of them for hours clearly excessive and injurious. Again, as before the enactment of the law, Mrs. Kelley wrote, "Little girls just fourteen years of age may be employed twenty consecutive hours, as they actually are in establishments known to the inspectors."

With this decision of the Supreme Court of Illinois, Mrs. Kelley entered upon her lifelong mission of interpreting the effects of court decisions upon American life.

Here was a subject seemingly unintelligible to the layman. It was a mark of Florence Kelley's early maturity that in 1895, when even to question the pronouncements of judges seemed "anarchistic," she should undertake to criticize the decision of this highest court of the state and to make clear the evil results flowing from its action. Far ahead of her time, she was convinced that people would have to understand this great issue—the nullification of labor laws by the courts —before it could be successfully met.

"There is no reasonable ground, at least none which has been made manifest to us in the argument of counsel for fixing eight hours in one day as the limit," said the court.

[8] See Chapter 11.

"The court was naturally not in a position to investigate the conditions of work in the factories and workshops of Illinois," rejoined the Chief Inspector of Factories. "That is not its function. But the legislature of 1893, which enacted the statute . . . had been in a position to investigate the conditions of manufacture throughout the state." Had she not herself accompanied the legislative committee appointed to make the investigation? They had thoroughly canvassed the subject and had decided that "in view of the intensity of the work and the speed required in virtually all occupations," eight hours constituted a limit beyond which women could not work without injury.

"All this," said Mrs. Kelley, "no court can do. It has no apparatus for such investigations; but this circumstance did not prevent the Illinois court from usurping the right."

The young woman who could, at the age of thirty-six, see thus clearly and express thus fearlessly an issue of profound implications to our national life, would go far in her subsequent exposure of reactionary courts and judicial decisions.

Governor Altgeld's term of office expired in 1897. He was succeeded by a Republican who promptly appointed, to replace Florence Kelley, a man who had been for twenty-seven years on the payroll of the Illinois Glass Company at Alton.

Mrs. Kelley remained at Hull House for the next two years. She was much in demand as a speaker, she was engaged in writing, and she had a position at the John Crerar Library where she was in charge in the evenings. It is of this period that Alice Hamilton gives an entertaining glimpse in her autobiography. A small group of residents would wait up for Mrs. Kelley on her return from the library and bribe her with hot chocolate to tell them of her experiences, for her rare gifts as a *raconteuse* gave to the most ordinary incidents of life sparkle and fire—how much more to the dramatic occurrences of the past few years in which she had been the leading figure. Andrew Bruce, who had been attor-

ney for the factory inspection department, lived at Hull
House and might also be present at the evening chocolate
drinking. "We had to be careful; foolish questions, half-
baked opinions, sentimental attitudes, met with no mercy
at her hands," writes Dr. Hamilton. "We loved to hear her
and the Scotch lawyer, Andrew Alexander Bruce, discuss
the cases they had had under the Altgeld administration." [9]

The time would soon come for Mrs. Kelley to leave Chicago where she had taken up life anew, where she had
formed lasting ties with those who remained ever after her
spiritual kindred, and where she had developed from ardent
propagandist to a practical administrator of high standing.
But a propagandist in the best sense of the word she would
remain to the end of her life, serving great causes. She would
always think of Hull House and her room there "overlooking the little court with its fountain," not nostalgically—for
she was born to look forward—but as one of the sources
from which she had drunk deep. Her nearly eight years there
had taught her much to add to her own personal experiences,
of good and evil, of all manner of personal relationships.

And most perhaps she felt that she had gained from living with Jane Addams. With her she felt most completely
in sympathy; in her she felt a spiritual power—the power of
one who sees life in spiritual terms. In the wave of reaction
after World War I, Miss Addams, like Mrs. Kelley, was to
know years of misrepresentation and slander. Indeed, from
the beginnings of Hull House she had experienced, besides
wide recognition, opposition of the most determined kind.
No one could fail to meet antagonism who spent her life as
she did in defending lost causes or causes which seemed
lost but which in the whirligig of time came to be accepted.
Hull House for years was to many synonymous with an-
archism, bolshevism, or whatever terms of opprobrium were
current at the time. But such was the power of Jane Addams'
personality, that gradually, as decade succeeded decade,

[9] *Exploring the Dangerous Trades* (Boston, 1943), p. 62.

she became perhaps more universally revered than any other living woman. Florence Kelley, as a socialist, differed with her economic views; but she loved Jane Addams and was more deeply influenced by her than by any other contemporary.

Next to Miss Addams, Mrs. Kelley would miss most, on leaving Hull House, companionship with Julia Lathrop. Lively differences of opinion existed between these two on some subjects. Miss Addams speaks somewhere of the "long and scintillating discussions between them, not only when both were residents but long afterwards when they often met there." Julia Lathrop, like Florence Kelley, had served her apprenticeship in the first years of Hull House. She had been a volunteer visitor for the Cook County agency in charge of relief, investigating all cases within ten blocks of Hull House. But no one was ever a "case" to her compassionate and humorous eye; and in her close acquaintance with the needs and fate of the very poor she gained that consummate knowledge of human nature which distinguished her later career as a member of the Illinois State Board of Charities and as first chief of the Children's Bureau in Washington. The Illinois board had supervision over the state institutions for the aged, the poor, the insane, etc. It spent two and a half million dollars yearly and made many thousands of appointments. The "spoils system" was rampant, and against this system Julia Lathrop exerted all her shrewd powers.

A discerning comparison between Julia Lathrop and Florence Kelley is worth quoting:

Mrs. Kelley was a fighter; Miss Lathrop was a diplomat. Both were brilliant, imaginative, humorous, and troubled by injustice. But Miss Lathrop had endless patience; Mrs. Kelley a kind of fiercely joyous impatience. Miss Lathrop glowed with determination. Mrs. Kelley burned with eagerness. . . . The logical, disciplined minds of both were accompanied by gentleness in Miss Lathrop, and high spiritedness in Mrs. Kelley.

Even their wit was different; one flashed, the other scorched.

When both were at Hull House together, arguing some problem of correcting a social injustice, and disagreeing as they often did on the best method of procedure, it is doubtful if any better talk was to be heard anywhere. Prime ministers of Europe, philosophers of all doctrines, labor leaders and great capitalists and unpopular poets and popular novelists and shabby exiles from half the kingdoms of the world visited Hull House and dined there and listened willingly. . . . And if they had only known it, in the "house meetings" afterwards which only residents attended, they would have heard more vivid discussions still, sternly practical, yet still enlivened by the same patient or impatient humor, as the case might be.[10]

[10] James Weber Linn, *Jane Addams, A Biography* (New York, 1935), p. 139.

Chapter 5

Consumers Organize for Action

Into the congenial group of Hull House residents there came, in 1899, a special visitor for Mrs. Kelley. He was John Graham Brooks, a well-known lecturer and writer from Cambridge, Massachusetts. He had come to invite Florence Kelley to go to New York City and head a new organization known as the National Consumers League.

The National Consumers League had been founded in 1899. It was the natural outgrowth of a movement which began in New York City eight years earlier, which had spread to other cities—Boston, Philadelphia, Brooklyn, Chicago—and which now needed a more general, unifying organization, under a competent executive. Florence Kelley's administration of the Illinois factory law, especially in enforcing the child labor and homework provisions, had brought her more than a local reputation. Here, then, was a woman extraordinarily well equipped to head a new organization designed to bring the power of consumers to bear upon the improvement of working conditions.

The Consumers League movement had started modestly enough. In 1891 a young working woman, Alice Woodbridge, employed in a large New York department store, sought help for the "girls behind the counter" from a prominent New York civic worker, Josephine Shaw Lowell. Mrs.

Lowell was the widow of Charles Russell Lowell and the
sister of Robert Gould Shaw, both of whom had given their
lives in the Civil War, and Mrs. Lowell had carried over
into social welfare causes the high traditions of her New England inheritance. In New York she stood for all that was
best in the civic and charitable life of the day. She was the
first woman to be appointed to the influential State Board
of Charities, she founded the Charity Organization Society,
and she now turned her interest to the hardships of working
girls.

Alice Woodbridge's facts, presented in a voice remembered for its moving beauty, carried conviction first to a
small group of women invited by Mrs. Lowell to hear her,
and later to a large public gathering in New York. She described life in department stores, a story then new to her
leisure-class audience: the excessively long hours unlimited
by law, the low wages often reduced by fines to the vanishing point, the threat to morals from unscrupulous employers
and floorwalkers, the injuries due to long standing, the extreme youth of children employed as "cash girls" and "cash
boys." Almost laughable in retrospect seems the "Standard
of a Fair House" set up as a goal by the new organization
which was formed, calling itself the Consumers League. To
throw the weight of their influence in favor of such employers "as deal justly by their employees," a list of "fair" department stores was compiled to which members of the League
were to give preference in shopping, a device later adopted
with varying degrees of success in other trades. But the
minimum wage recommended, below which no store could
fall, in this first trial, was actually $6 weekly for experienced
saleswomen and $2 for cash girls.[1]

However feeble the beginning, a new movement had

---

[1] It is true that the cost of living at that time was low as compared
with ours. The League's own investigation of living costs for working
girls itself came to no more than $8 per week. But even then the dif-
ference of 25 per cent between the two figures was crucial. See p. 65.

been launched. A third party in industry, the consuming public, had been recognized. The power of the consumer and the responsibility that power entailed were made explicit. John Graham Brooks, the first president of the League, put the case for the new movement in a nutshell: "This is the economic truth," he declared. "To buy a sweated garment is to have someone work for you under sweated conditions as definitely as if she were in your own employ." In the same way, to buy goods from stores such as those Alice Woodbridge described was to condone the working conditions they provided and to help perpetuate them.

What could a small group of consumers do about it? Education sometimes seems the slowest of human processes, but after a half-century which has brought a revolution in social aims and methods, widespread education through a presentation of facts remains an indispensable method of effecting change in a democratic society. It was such education to which the Consumers League addressed itself. Its media were simple indeed compared to the modern paraphernalia of publicity. But its members were not naive. From the beginning they recognized that consumer persuasion would not be enough. They saw that new laws would be needed too, and they consistently worked for them.

During its first five years of existence, the New York Consumers League worked to have department store employees, like factory workers, protected by legislation. At that time, women employed in factories were covered by a ten-hour law, but for department store employees there was no limitation of hours whatever. During the Christmas season, overtime, often until midnight, was regularly required without extra pay, and often with consequent exhaustion and illness. By 1896 enough public interest had been aroused to result in appointment of a legislative investigating commission known as the Reinhard Commission. Facts which the Consumers League joined in presenting to the commission induced that body to recommend the first mercantile hour law for New York. It was passed the same year, but it disappointed the high hopes of its proponents. For enforcement of the new law was placed in the hands of local boards of health which had neither appropriations, personnel, nor the desire to make the law operative. Not until 1908, after years of further agitation, was enforcement of the Mercantile Act given over to the proper authority, the New York State Labor Department.

In 1896 Mrs. Lowell retired from the presidency and was followed by Mrs. Frederick Nathan, who remained the able head of the New York Consumers League for a quarter-century.

New projects undertaken during these early years which became permanently associated with the name of the Consumers League were the early Christmas shopping campaign, a forlorn hope for decades; the establishment of the Saturday half-holiday in stores, and some provision for seats for saleswomen. "My store is not a hospital," had been the classic response of a department store head to the demand for seats, as brought out at a hearing of the Reinhard Commission.

In 1898 a new call came to the League which had wide repercussions. A strike and lock-out occurred in the ladies' tailoring industry. Responding to appeals from some of the workers, the League undertook to investigate. The chief evil found was the general practice of sending out even the most expensive garments to be finished in the living quarters of tenement workers, with all the dangers inseparable from tenement homework.

The gargantuan task of establishing a "white list" of tailors, that is, of those who did not send out garments to be finished in the tenements, seemed impossible for a volunteer body such as the Consumers League. There was a New York law at that time requiring the licensing of workers for homework, but it had never been enforced and, as Mrs.

Kelley was soon to demonstrate, it was indeed unenforceable.

The Consumers League did succeed in arousing considerable publicity as to the tailoring strike and what lay behind it. Governor Theodore Roosevelt came down from Albany to see sweatshop conditions for himself; and after a tour of the tenements, urged, in his message to the legislature in 1898, that a law similar to that of Massachusetts be adopted. This required that *buildings* used for manufacturing purposes must be licensed, instead of the individual workers.

Meantime the Consumers League movement had spread to other cities. Mrs. Nathan was invited, as the president of the first league, to speak in various other cities. The next two leagues were formed in Brooklyn and in Philadelphia.

In 1897 John Graham Brooks was instrumental in forming leagues in Boston and in Chicago (where he undoubtedly saw Mrs. Kelley at Hull House). Mr. Brooks lived in Boston but traveled widely in his firsthand study of labor conditions and social movements. A man of great personal charm, he was in demand as a speaker on such subjects and was able to do much to promote the Consumers League idea. The new Massachusetts League, it may be noted in passing, engaged as its first investigator of Boston department stores in 1898 a young man named W. L. MacKenzie King, who later served for many years as Canada's prime minister.

The logic of events turned the interests of the Massachusetts League from conditions in department stores to conditions in factories. As early as May, 1898, the Massachusetts group suggested a conference to consider the possibility of federating the various local leagues. The object of the new federation would be to extend the movement and also to establish some method for guaranteeing that goods had been manufactured, as well as sold, under proper working conditions. The New York League, following its experience in the tailors' strike, was also eager to expand its work into this new field.

The conscientious consumer, these women believed, did not want to buy goods manufactured in substandard factories or finished in tenements, even though sold in stores which had satisfactory working conditions. But how could the consumer know what goods to avoid? Here it was felt the league should take a hand. Better factories, like better stores, might be recommended for preference by having their products marked with a label guaranteeing that they had been produced under good working conditions. David against Goliath indeed! How could the Consumers League induce manufacturers to qualify for or use such a label? These women resolved to try. To keep the experiment within manageable limits, they decided to begin with one small industry—women's and children's white cotton underwear.

In this industry there were no unions, hence no union label. Even in industries which used the union label, it furnished guarantees as to hours and wages but did not cover the sanitary conditions in the factories or their use of child labor or of outside tenement work. How could a Consumers League label give a guarantee of decent working conditions, including all these various matters? This was the main topic for discussion at a first conference of delegates from six leagues in May, 1898. Mrs. Kelley was the delegate from Illinois. At this meeting a constitution for the proposed federation was drawn up and preliminaries agreed upon for a label on guaranteed goods. In January, 1899, these proposals were ratified at a second meeting in New York; the name, National Consumers League was adopted; Mr. Brooks was elected president and Mrs. Kelley appointed general secretary.

On coming to New York in May, 1899, Mrs. Kelley immediately proceeded on the two-fold program before her: to stimulate the growth of the Consumers League and to inspect cotton underwear factories for the label. She traced

out, then and there, the pattern she was to follow for many
a year. This is not to say that she did not continually vary
and broaden it as time went on. But in her second annual
report, for 1900, she shows in a sentence how large a conception underlay her work from the outset.

"Taken in its widest sense, the work of the Consumers
League is an educational movement as all-embracing as the
need of civilized people for food, clothing and shelter."

Mrs. Kelley's official title was general secretary of the
National Consumers League. Actually she was the driving
force of a society comparatively small in number and loose
in organization, but effective out of all proportion to its
size or financial resources. Whatever its weaknesses, it gave
to Mrs. Kelley what she most needed to function effectively;
it gave her the one thing without which she could not have
developed as she did, without which she could not live: it
gave her freedom. Aside from the perennial lack of funds,
a lack which she magnificently disregarded ("where would
we be if I waited for funds!" she would exclaim), she was
free to initiate, to invent new methods, to throw herself
into whatever issue seemed paramount, with no more for-
malities of procedure than she chose to observe, and with
the enthusiastic support of a scattered but coherent following. She engaged in a wide variety of campaigns—against
child labor, tenement sweatshops, starvation wages, excessive hours. Somehow she had a genius for keeping all the
balls in the air at the same time. She was a guerrilla warrior.
In the wilderness of industrial wrongs she would move first
against one injustice then another, whichever seemed at the
moment most accessible to attack.

Year after year Florence Kelley traveled the length and
breadth of the land without any remotely adequate living
allowance, earning her way by fees large and small, no
penny of which she ever dreamed of considering personal
income, though her salary might be weeks in arrears. She
inspired a devoted following over a wide territory; of course

she also aroused antagonism. No one as forthright as she, as unsparing in attack and as implacable against her opponents, could fail to make enemies. Her great qualities cannot obliterate her faults—her high temper, her impatience, and her tendency never to forget or forgive opposition. Men and women alike were, understandably enough, often afraid of her. Even Alice Hamilton, her lifelong friend, writes of first meeting her as "that vivid, colorful, rather frightening personality whom I later came to adore."

To spread the Consumers League movement and to spy out the land for appropriate label factories demanded an inordinate amount of travel. At the close of her first year, though she was still feeling her way and was, moreover, prevented from speaking from March to May by an attack of diphtheria, Mrs. Kelley lists speeches made by her in ten different states and the District of Columbia before national, state, and local groups. In her report for 1903 she lists the formidable total of 111 meetings which she had addressed in fifteen different states, and she illustrates the diversity of her audiences in a two-day visit to Pittsburgh. There she had spoken to the local league, to the Ladies Catholic Benevolent Association, and to "Wimodaughsis," an organization of the wives, mothers, and daughters of Master Masons. She took infinite satisfaction in the diversity of her audiences and addressed herself to each with the skill of the born orator, differentiating her approach almost by instinct.

She was always at the call of any local league that needed her, for meetings large or small, or for legislative hearings or conferences. She would stay a week or more at a time, speaking two or three times a day. How the leagues responded to that dynamic impulse can be seen by an extract from an early report from Massachusetts. Mrs. Kelley was the great asset for them all: "Our national secretary who can address us every day in the week, giving us each time new facts and suggestions, who can travel from one end of the Continent to the other without losing her hold upon local problems in state leagues the farthest removed from her bodily presence, stirring our zeal and opening new fields for our activity by letters which are as prompt and full as if letter-writing were the chief occupation of her day."

At the end of the first year 5 new state leagues had been formed, in New Jersey, Minnesota, Ohio, Michigan, and Wisconsin, besides new local leagues in New York and Pennsylvania. The next year there were 30 leagues in eleven states; at the close of the fifth year, 64 leagues in twenty states.

Some of these leagues languished and died, but they were replaced by others. Mrs. Kelley, while always a vital stimulant even to feeble organizations, was never an effective organizer. Indeed, the truth is that she had no talent for administration. She never devised any consistent patterns of development for the local leagues and their work had to depend, largely, on their own initiative and methods. Mrs. Kelley's remarkable flair for finding and enlisting people of unusual ability and character, both in her own national league and in the state and local leagues, was her strongest asset.

Representatives of the leagues met at the annual meetings and agreed upon general policies; and a smaller group met quarterly to compare notes and struggle with perennial difficulties as to funds. The group was small because the local and even the state leagues were often too poor to send delegates. Yet, however small, these meetings were significant, because of the presence always of a handful of people who had firsthand knowledge of working conditions in their localities and were determined to right them. In cooperation with labor organizations and the very few like-minded groups then existing, the local and state consumers' leagues succeeded, over the years, in achieving a remarkable record. Through their efforts a substantial body of protective legislation was enacted; their continued watchful interest was immensely valuable in promoting adequate enforcement.

In her very first year with the Consumers League, Mrs. Kelley began her educational work in colleges and universities, speaking at the universities of Chicago and Wisconsin, Brown and Syracuse, at Wellesley, Vassar, and Packer Institute, and before various college clubs. She greatly valued this objective and intellectual backing of her program.

"The cooperation of the professors of Economics at Harvard, Yale, Columbia, Cornell, Michigan, Chicago, and Pennsylvania, in serving as honorary vice-presidents, has been of incalculable value in silencing criticism—and in giving confidence in the soundness of the basis upon which the work of the League is founded," she wrote in 1902.[2]

She not only valued the faculty backing but also the opportunity to enlist the students, as she well knew she could. No journey was too excessive to reach these young people, and no opportunity to address them was lost. As she once said, "Sometimes a single girl on returning home becomes the nucleus of work in a whole state."

One of the generation of students whom she was to awaken to lifelong service put into vivid words what Mrs. Kelley had meant to those college audiences:

There are many women in this audience today [said Frances Perkins at a memorial meeting], whose first knowledge of Florence Kelley came when they were young women in college or in school, when she didn't find it too much trouble to journey on a night sleeper in the dead of winter to a small New England town where there was a little handful of girls studying economics or sociology who thought they would be glad to hear from her.

She was willing to go into these little far corners where a handful of girls were students and tell them about the program which she was evolving for industrial and human and social justice. And that influence which she had over a whole generation was of extreme significance. She took a whole group of young people, formless in their aspirations and molded their aspirations for social justice into some definite purpose, into a

[2] Florence Kelley, Annual Report dated March 4, 1902, unpublished.

program that had meaning and that had experience and that had practicality back of it.[3]

The second part of Mrs. Kelley's early program was the label for white goods. Today, employers and unions in the garment trades enforce prohibition of tenement work through collective bargaining, and such work has been prohibited by state and federal law in many branches of manufacture. Today, children under sixteen years are not wanted as factory employees, and their employment is prohibited by the laws of most states and by the federal Fair Labor Standards Act. So today the label of the National Consumers League on white goods and its guarantee may seem both naive and negligible. But in 1900 it was neither. It was a bold step, far in advance of the laws and practices of the time. For among the requirements for obtaining the label were two provisos which then and for decades thereafter were nothing less than revolutionary; they obtained in no other industry.[4] These were the total prohibition of the work of children under sixteen years, and the prohibition of tenement homework. No goods might bear the label which had not been fully completed upon the employers' premises.

The third requirement for using the label, namely, that all state laws were being observed in the plant, gave Mrs. Kelley a weapon for gauging the performance of state factory inspectors which she found highly useful.

To attack at their source the twin evils of child labor and homework which she hated with an almost personal fervor, in a field that was small but thereby the more manageable, was an undertaking after Mrs. Kelley's own heart. To it she applied herself with gusto.

At the close of her first year she could write that she

---

[3] Frances Perkins, speech at a memorial meeting in honor of Florence Kelley held at the Friends Meeting House in New York City, March 16, 1932.

[4] Except for the sixteen-year minimum age in mining.

had obtained information concerning "all the important and virtually all the unimportant sources of supply of the white muslin underwear produced in this country." She had succeeded in finding fifteen factories whose product could be guaranteed as made in accordance with the label, and had persuaded those employers to affix the label to their products. She had investigated many more whose skepticism of its commercial value led them to refuse to use the label; and another class to whom, owing to bad conditions, it could not be granted. In New York the methods of the state factory department were found to be such that no guarantee could be given that the law was obeyed or that goods were completed on the premises. Mrs. Kelley's long campaign against tenement homework in New York I reserve for fuller description in a later chapter.

Along with getting factories to use the Consumers League label, Mrs. Kelley had to create a demand for it among the purchasers of cotton underwear. Would enough women take the trouble to ask for and insist upon getting these special garments? To persuade their members and friends to buy enough of these goods to make them commercially profitable became one of the main activities of the local leagues.

At that time, more than forty years ago, the era of silk, rayon, and nylon underwear was still far in the future. Fine hand-embroidered underwear imported from France was available, and dainty cambric garments made in this country. But these were too often finished in the tenements. While the label factories made some fine goods, on the whole their products were not designed on esthetic lines, and a considerable sense of virtue was needed to sustain the wearers of the voluminous nightgowns, chemises, and other underwear of the period made of heavy, often coarse, white cotton. "Absolutely heroic" is the praise accorded to their members for their devotion to principle in using these garments, in an early report of the Consumers League of Maryland.

The label, however, in the fifteen years of its existence served its purpose. It was a valuable educational device, giving to the consumers a concrete task to do, and proving that a considerable body of women could be counted on to put their principles into practice at the cost of personal inconvenience. If the better showing of New England in pushing the label was due partly to the Puritan conscience of the wearers in resisting the more attractive and frivolous garments, it was due also to the higher labor standards of Massachusetts in particular. By 1904, sixteen of the thirty-eight label factories were located in Massachusetts, where labor laws and enforcement alike were in advance of any other state.

Ten years later, Mrs. Kelley had succeeded in establishing a list of seventy manufacturers making a wide variety of women's and children's cotton garments who used the Consumers League label. But she was not satisfied. The label factories could be guaranteed to provide decent sanitary conditions and hours of work and some protection against child labor, for these were legal standards in various states; and she could check to some extent how well the laws were enforced. But what of wages? During the first decade of the century no American state had any law to provide a "floor" for wages. Increasingly, Mrs. Kelley felt that without a minimum wage the League's other guarantees were of little value. Poverty was the most inclusive ill, from which stemmed ever-widening injuries to the workers, physical, social, and economic. With her instinct for getting at the root of difficulties, she felt more and more strongly the need for attacking poverty at its source in substandard wages. "We have slowly become convinced," she wrote, "that low wages produce more poverty than all other causes together."

Because the label did not guarantee fair wages, did not even afford any means of turning the light upon wages

(which remained the "private business" of the employer),
it was felt to have outlived its usefulness. It had indeed become a source of keen anxiety to Florence Kelley. She felt
the anomaly of continuing to recommend goods made under
conditions of pay which she could not even scrutinize, much
less guarantee as satisfactory. What was the minimum required for decent living, either for girls living away
from home or for those helping in family support? How
many worked solely for "pin-money" as was complacently
assumed? Anxiously the council of the League debated these
new and unanswered questions at more than one meeting.
Could there be a minimum wage for the whole country or
for a whole state? For city and for rural districts alike? The
debates ended in bewilderment. Forty years ago, it must be
reiterated, when Mrs. Kelley began to agitate these questions, not only was no information in hand but there were
few relevant precedents to follow in seeking the facts.

Casting about for means to light the darkness of that
period, Mrs. Kelley enthusiastically backed the demand
stemming from Illinois for a federal investigation of all
phases of women's employment.[5] In 1906 she was urging
all the consumers' leagues, now numbering over 60 in twenty
states, to work for this bill. It was passed by Congress in
1907 and in the course of time a nineteen-volume report was
published which gave important new information.

Not content to await this report, Mrs. Kelley, also in
1906, persuaded her own organization to make a modest inquiry of its own. To this inquiry she assigned Sue B. Ainslie
of her staff, who devoted to it most of the next two years.
Days and evenings were spent interviewing working girls
and getting from them, at regular intervals, authentic records of what they had spent.

A little volume called *Making Both Ends Meet*, embodying the results of Miss Ainslie's reports, and written by

---

[5] The lead was taken by the Illinois Women's Trade Union League
and the Illinois Consumers League.

Edith Wyatt of Chicago, was published in 1908—one of the earliest reliable sources of information on the cost of living for working girls and women. Without taking into account items today recognized as essential, such as saving for medical and dental care, insurance, some forms of recreation, etc., the bare minimum arrived at was $8 per week. After twenty years of agitation the New York Consumers League had induced between 50 and 60 retail merchants to pay to women over eighteen years of age not less than $6 per week.

"So grave a discrepancy between the need of the workers and the minimum wage attained in 20 years of persuasion calls for new and more effective ways of compelling payment of a living wage," wrote Florence Kelley sharply. "So long as women's wages rest upon the assumption that every woman has a husband, father, brother or lover contributing to her support, so long these sinister incidents of women's industrial employment (tuberculosis, insanity, vice) are inevitable."

What new weapon could be devised to raise or even to disclose the meager pay of girls and women in the trades not protected by collective bargaining?

Chapter 6

Henry Street and Summers in Maine

When Mrs. Kelley came to New York, she did not attempt to set up a household of her own but went to live with Lillian Wald at the Nurses Settlement on Henry Street, later known as the Henry Street Settlement. The house was unique among settlements because it grew out of the nursing work of its founder, one of the great modern figures in the ancient profession of nursing. It was chance that had led Lillian Wald into the tenements as a newly graduated, ardent young nurse in 1893, but it was not chance that kept her for a lifetime at the work of seeking to rectify what she found there. It was her conviction that sickness, poverty, reeking tenements, ignorance were things that could and must be remedied. With that love for all human kind which was at the core of her being, she moved at once with a friend into the lower East Side, then unredeemed as it has since been from some of its worst evils, and began her career of nursing and education, and of bringing beauty into the sordidness of the world about her.

In Lillian Wald, Florence Kelley found an ally in all the causes for which she was on fire when she came from Chicago: the protection of childhood, first of all; the fight against the sweatshop, against labor abuses of all sorts, against poverty and ignorance. Lillian Wald and Henry

Street in New York were to mean for Florence Kelley what Jane Addams and Hull House had meant to her in Chicago. Here, again, she was in the midst of the stream of life "in that back room at 265 Henry Street where one hears the constant roar of Grand Street and the lower East Side." Here, again, she learned at first hand the lot of human beings less fortunately situated, subjected to pressures seeming sometimes unendurable, yet borne with fortitude, often with gaiety.

Lillian Wald, like Florence Kelley, was concerned about the *causes* of the evils she combatted. To nurse the sick was the primary function of nursing, but the time had come, Miss Wald thought, for nurses to widen their scope. A new aspect of medical science at this period was its growing stress on prevention of sickness, on teaching people how to keep well; and in the visiting nurse the new public health movement found its most effective field agent. It was this aspect of nursing—the teaching of hygiene in the home, whether in the case of babies, or of the tubercular or the convalescent, or of the handicapped shut-in or the chronic invalid—that Lillian Wald was among the first to stress.

In all these developments Florence Kelley took the keenest interest. Along these lines, she felt, was hope for the future.[1] The nurses shared a special kind of intimacy with the whole neighborhood, an intimacy in which Mrs. Kelley participated and from which she drew the human facts on which her thinking was based. While she was among the first to develop the resources of more formal social research, she valued equally the informal, daily, revealing contacts of the settlement. Lillian Wald was herself the magnet who drew to her house on Henry Street all sorts and conditions of men, women, and children, from Downtown and from Uptown Manhattan, and from every country on earth, it some-

---

[1] Equally hopeful for children of school age was Lillian Wald's demonstration in 1902 (first in the United States) of the value of the school nurse, soon taken over by the city and later established in all the states of the union and in many countries of the world.

times seemed. There was a buoyancy and outgoing warmth about her which few could resist. Florence Kelley could say of her what she had said of Jane Addams—that all the world came sooner or later to her door.

There were other settlement workers in New York with whom Mrs. Kelley was soon on intimate terms. Among these I must mention especially John L. Elliott and Mary K. Simkhovitch, who, like her, saw in industrial conditions the root cause of misery and unrest. Their common interests soon led to deep-seated and lifelong friendships. Another co-worker and lifelong friend was the New York lawyer George W. Alger, a leader in the New York Child Labor Committee.[2]

And in the so-called Charities Building at Twenty-second Street and Fourth Avenue, where she had her office, there were gradually congregated the colleagues with whom she was to be associated in a variety of new social movements, unknown before 1900. It was a time of intellectual and educational ferment. I well remember the day Charles Spahr, who was on the staff of the old *Outlook*,[3] then a prominent weekly publication, put his head into the doorway of the assembly hall on the first floor and saw collected there the well-known figures of the building: Edward T. Devine, the head of the Charity Organization Society, whose vision led to the extension of relief into constructive tenement house reform and tuberculosis work; Lawrence Veiller, then head of these new divisions of the Charity Organization Society; Samuel McCune Lindsay and Owen Lovejoy of the new National Child Labor Committee; George Hall of the recent New York Child Labor Committee; Mrs. Kelley and others

[2] When Mr. Alger heard of this biography, he wrote in a letter: "I only hope the life . . . does not make Mrs. Kelley an institution rather than a person. She never was an institution to me, but a very real, thrilling and delightful woman and one of my best friends for many decades."

[3] The publication, which (to our amazement) Theodore Roosevelt had joined as a contributing editor on his return from Africa in 1910, occupied a floor of the Charities Building.

of the national and state consumers' leagues; Paul and Arthur Kellogg of the *Survey* and *Survey Graphic,* then the little sheet known as *Charities.*

"Ah," exclaimed Charles Spahr genially, "what's this bunch call itself today?" In point of fact, this was a meeting of the new American Association for Labor Legislation which John R. Commons had come from Wisconsin to introduce in New York, and which, under John B. Andrews, was soon to make the first American investigation into industrial poisoning, the dreaded "phossy-jaw" among phosphorus match workers.

In all these organizations Florence Kelley was a dynamic influence. But her closest associates, and nearest to her heart, were the editors of *Charities,* the little publication, then scarcely more than a social worker's house organ or trade journal, which was to become the *Survey Graphic,* a highly valuable organ of public opinion on national social issues. She was a contributing editor, and her influence on the magazine was great. As Editor Paul Kellogg once said, "She personified, more than anything else, the quickening of women's concern for the humanizing of industry in this epoch of change." He said he always knew, when he heard laughter break out in the next room, that Mrs. Kelley had come over from the League offices. "It did not matter how grim an indictment she might be forging for our pages at the time. . . . That was the way with her—wrath and gaiety kindling from the same inner flame."

It was during these early years in New York, in 1905, that a tragedy befell Mrs. Kelley which overshadowed her life for years. This was the sudden death, from a heart attack, of her teen-age daughter Margaret shortly after she had entered Smith College. The three children had lived with their mother at Henry Street or with friends nearby until they went away to school or college.

Margaret Kelley had grown into a handsome and vigorous young woman, alert, willful, adoring and adored by her mother. She had spent the last two years of her life in Boston preparing for college in the home of her mother's close friend, Mrs. Glendower Evans.

Mrs. Kelley took every opportunity that offered to visit Margaret at Mrs. Evans' house. She could see her older son Nicholas at the same time, since he was then at Harvard. And at Christmas time she brought her younger son John, so that the four were united under Mrs. Evans' roof, to the great satisfaction of that generous and impulsive person.

A telegram received shortly after Margaret had entered Smith College brought her mother the incredible news of Margaret's sudden death. Lillian Wald immediately joined the bereft mother at Northampton and took her for a week's recuperation in the Berkshire Hills. I remember the shock of Mrs. Kelley's appearance on her return. She looked years older, her face was set. She plunged into work as though possessed by a fever of activity, as though work was all that was left to her.

I accompanied her shortly afterward to a hearing before the New York City Board of Estimate on a much disputed school budget. Various speakers had put forward arguments for and against extended school activities before Mrs. Kelley rose to speak. In her black dress, her face a tragic mask, some emanation of her grief seemed to hang about her. She seemed to those who knew of her loss the embodiment of a tragic Niobe; and her plea for the children was made in tones so deep and haunting that complete silence fell on the crowded room. Her voice broke near the end, and she took her seat abruptly. But the silence continued, and with no further words the hearing was over. "What has happened to Mrs. Kelley?" more than one person queried anxiously as I followed her up the aisle.

But nature, pushed too far, rebelled. For some weeks after the hearing, even that grim determination had to yield to physical disability. For some weeks Mrs. Kelley was obliged to drop her work, even to stay in bed for a while.

There was one incident that aroused her during that sad period. The first copy of her book, *Some Ethical Gains Through Legislation,* was delivered by her publisher. The manuscript had been completed during the previous summer of 1904. She had worked long and arduously upon it. She seized eagerly upon that first copy of her book. It was like a clarion call back to the causes which her grief had blotted out. It summed up her whole philosophy of action: the right to carefree childhood, the right of the worker to leisure, the right of the purchaser to sanitary merchandise, the rights of women to the ballot, all illustrated by a wealth of concrete facts derived from her life's experiences. "But chiefly," as she said in the Preface, "as a resident for thirteen years beginning in 1892, first at Hull House in Chicago and afterwards at the Nurses' Settlement in New York."

Mrs. Kelley's grief over the daughter she had lost deepened her interest in other young women, whom she was always happy to help and advise. As she wrote to one of them who had asked what would be the best preparation for work she wanted to do: "It gives me the greatest possible pleasure to hear from you. Remember that I have no daughter to write to me, and do it whenever you can."

No doubt her deep maternal instinct was the driving power behind her lifelong crusade for child labor laws, for the U. S. Children's Bureau, and for infant and maternity aid. But along with this powerful love for children in the mass was an ever-ready concern for individual children. She responded to their needs without limit or thought of self. In 1913, when she was returning from Europe, the steamer she was on—the "Kroonland"—was one of three which came to the rescue of the "Volturno," which was on fire in mid-ocean. In the confusion, some families became separated. Three babies were brought aboard the "Kroonland" whose parents had been taken to other ships. Among all the passengers, it was Florence Kelley who took charge of these babies.

For those who never saw Florence Kelley face to face
or heard her speak, it is hard to convey the dynamic quality
of her personality—the power within her which, combined
with her keen intellect and tireless energy, made her so re-
markably effective.

When I first saw her, shortly after she came to New
York to become general secretary of the Consumers League,
she was forty years old. She was built on large lines, her
head crowned with heavy braids of beautiful dark hair. Her
dark eyes looked out on the tragi-comedy of life with a
direct and fearless gaze. Her face was mobile in the extreme, changing with each mood. She had a wide generous
mouth which quivered like a child's when she was moved
and, at the least provocation of her keen sense of humor,
broke out into her broad infectious smile. She had pre-
eminently the speaker's gift. At her best she was unrivaled.
No other man or woman whom I have ever heard so blended
knowledge of facts, wit, satire, burning indignation, prophetic denunciation—all poured out at white heat in a voice
varying from flute-like tones to deep organ tones. She had the
great gift of brevity, and having made her point would often
stop abruptly, leaving her audience shaken. Or when her
opponents at a hearing or conference appeared to have carried the day, she would arise last, and beginning in the soft
silken tones which betokened her most dangerous mood,
adroitly and devastatingly turn the tables.

Mr. Alger recalls a hearing over the bill to transfer enforcement of department store regulations from local boards
of health to the New York Labor Department.[4] "One store
manager," writes Mr. Alger, "told Governor Hughes that the
transfer might disturb the very friendly relations now existing between the store and its employees. This made Mrs.
Kelley see red. When she got up she flayed each department
store separately. As to this one she said sarcastically, 'I, of
course appreciate your devotion to your employees and

[4] See Chapter 5.

theirs to you; but perhaps this transfer will have the effect of making you do something about the unventilated basement in which so many of your girls have acquired tuberculosis.' As to another store she said: 'Perhaps this transfer will make you rescind the rule which you now have, under which any girl who sits down in a chair, which a law now requires you to supply to these over-worked girls, will be discharged.' She had something separate on each one of them."[5]

Lillian Wald used to tell how once at a crowded hearing she overhead one indignant employer say to another: "You know this bill is all wrong, why don't you say something?" "What," replied the other, "and let that fire-eater in the black dress make a monkey of me!"

In her later years Florence Kelley compared in revealing words her own and John Fitch's response to the conditions found in the Pittsburgh Survey of 1907-08 in which they both took part. "I well remember," she wrote him, "how impatient I used to be eighteen long years ago, in Pittsburgh, because at that time your mind used to seem to me as clear and cool as a great French glass window. I was myself such a raging furnace, so consumed with burning indignation against everything that I saw and smelt and breathed and loathed, that I had no appreciation whatever of the merit of your power of insight and passionless statement of undistorted facts."

In this letter she did herself somewhat less than justice. In all the years I knew Florence Kelley, she did appreciate facts, and she wanted them completely undistorted. Whenever her indignation led her to inaccuracy or even to exaggeration, she welcomed correction. It was her unique quality and her great strength that she combined the scrupulous scholar and the passionate advocate.

Mrs. Kelley never set up a home of her own in New York. For many years she stuck to her cramped quarters and the noisy, gregarious life of Henry Street. She did not

---

[5] Personal letter from George W. Alger.

want personal possessions and their problems to distract her
from her work; and she knew that for her, at least, possessions, even beautiful ones, had little power to give real
satisfaction. Once she expressed her feeling in a letter to a
young assistant who also lived at Henry Street. She wrote
Marjorie Johnson from the latter's home in Madison, Wisconsin, where she was staying while on a speaking trip:

"If I had not spent the unhappiest years of my life in
very beautiful houses and the happiest years where I had—
like the Founder of our Religion—not a place to lay my
head, it would be hard for me to understand how you can
prefer your roost at 257 Henry Street to this beautiful and
charming home."

But for summer vacations she sought a place of her own.
Her winters were extremely strenuous, with constant traveling and the multitude of activities while in New York. She
had a finger in so many pies. Outside the Consumers League
and peripheral related activities, she was vice-president of
the National Woman Suffrage Association, was on the executive board of the Intercollegiate Socialist Society, later the
League for Industrial Democracy, and followed Socialist
party activities with keen interest. As she wrote in a letter in
1912, "Life is so interesting that it takes self-control to sleep
at night." We all urged her to take a regular six weeks' to
two months' vacation completely away from everything. She
looked for a place in a cool and bracing climate, for heat
she always found trying. Our office in New York was known
facetiously as the "cave of the winds," for neither of us could
tolerate the usual overheating of public buildings and always preferred flying papers to stifling steam heat.

In 1907 Mrs. Kelley found the refuge she sought on the
cold Maine Coast, with its chill fogs and hot noons, where
the salt of the sea and the forest air of spruce and pine
mingle so intoxicatingly. On the tip of Naskeag Point, jutting
out from the mainland into the waters known as Egge-
moggin Reach, she bought an old house and about ten acres

(to which she added year by year). It was a spot admirably suited to her needs, remote, not easily accessible from the outside world, yet within a mile of the little village of Brooklin. From her neighbors there she could procure needed supplies.

She often took with her a Negro woman and her child, to whom she became attached; or in other years a warm-hearted Irish girl who remained in her son's family several winters; or some other domestic helper. Domestic cares weighed lightly upon her. The house ran itself more or less in the easy American vacation mood. Mrs. Kelley usually worked in the mornings, writing articles and carrying on a substantial correspondence. Some summers she took her secretary with her for part of the season, or she would engage a girl to come for a few weeks to take dictation.

Of the multitude of people who knew Florence Kelley in her public life, on the platform, at meetings, in the settlements close to crowded humanity, few knew that part of her which craved the very opposite of her hectic routine. An inner need for solitude, for quiet, for the beauty of nature, for her own home, the Maine summers satisfied.

"I start tomorrow for Maine, heavenly thought. . . . Here summer goes on being heaven. . . . For three weeks here in an obscure fishing village, I have been enjoying almost perfect silence and exquisite beauty. . . . As you see from the letter-head, I have arrived in Fog Land and am to have, all told, seventy days of quiet here on my granite farm."

Casual expressions such as these in letters of successive summers betray the depth of her feeling for the Maine summers. Another year she writes a little more at length:

Yesterday and today it is Heaven here in the Northwest wind, looking out over the water and the woods and the fir-clad islands.

Helen and I are working on the south porch, and while I dictate I look at a hundred butterflies getting honey from the huge white fluffy blossoms of the only sumac of its kind that I have ever seen, an inheritance from the previous owner of the farm who lived here forty years. The bush is therefore well past sixty years old and as lusty as a bush can be.

In her actual ownership of these acres lay another un-suspected source of joy and refreshment. Was it because of the cramped quarters of her winters that she so rejoiced in space? Was it because she had so long been obliged to cut down on all personal belongings that, when the opportunity offered, she found in herself a deep desire for possessions? Year by year she bought more land, toward the end of her life even an island lying off-shore, to preserve her view and her privacy from possible encroachment. To her friends' teasing that a socialist and Henry Georgite now owned a hundred Maine acres, she smilingly assented. It was illogical, she knew, but she loved it.

Inherent in her ownership of the land was also the satis-faction of her sense of home. Here in contrast to her winter travel she could send down her roots. Here, as against the single bedrooms and the shared sociability of the settlement, however prized, she was hostess in her own right. All those deep instincts of home of her Quaker forebears and her Quaker childhood rose up within her. Now she could invite to her home one or the other of her sons or her grandchildren or a cherished friend.

She loved sailing and never refused the chance of a sail, however rough the water. She loved the sense of young life about her. The blueberry picking in which all must join was a household ritual. The berries clustered so thickly on the bushes that they could be raked off into pails, leaves and all, to be picked over later; and so bountiful is nature's growth in that cold fog-laden sea air with its hot noon sun that the supply seemed endless—too endless for some tastes, but never for the happy owner of these acres.

And again in her stormy moods, the Maine summers min-istered subtly to her spirit. The something that was ele-mental in her responded to the elemental in nature and fed upon it. She would go out into the driving rain of a stormy night when the wind was howling off the sea. The wildness, the cold gale sweeping in from the sea, the flying clouds were what she loved. She would come back later, blown, streaming, breathless, and exultant.

Thus that cold Maine Coast, alternately fog-drenched or sun-baked, blown upon by all the winds of heaven, gave to her stormy spirit that sense of identification with cosmic forces which is religion to many natures. Each year the six weeks in Maine fortified Florence Kelley for her strenuous winter program. Each year she came back to New York, her strength and zest renewed. As she herself described it once in her later years: "I am back at work with my battery recharged."

Chapter 7

The Crusade Against Child Labor

Florence Kelley's social concern was first aroused when, herself still a child, she saw small boys at work at night in steel mills and glass factories on those early memorable trips with her father. Throughout her life, child labor remained her first concern.

Prohibition of child labor was one of the basic standards of the first Consumers League label; and in her inspection of label factories Mrs. Kelley kept a wary eye out for child labor infractions. To broaden her work for children she accepted all invitations to serve other organizations willing to do any work in this field. She became chairman of the Child Labor Committee of the National Woman Suffrage Association and of the National Congress of Mothers, and a member of a similar committee of the General Federation of Women's Clubs. Thus she kept before these large groups of women a subject then highly controversial. At the turn of the century, agitation against the employment of young children in industry was just beginning in many parts of the country. In the South where northern capital was priming the rapid development of the textile industry, discussion of child labor was bitterly resented and there were virtually no child labor laws. Georgia had no age minimum whatsoever, or other restrictions on the employment of children;

Alabama and South Carolina set a minimum age of ten years; in North Carolina and Louisiana no child could be employed under twelve. Even in the northern industrial states of Pennsylvania and Rhode Island, the minimum age was thirteen. Moreover, in both South and North such child labor laws as existed were too often completely unenforced.

The Consumers League membership, though small, was widespread throughout both North and South, and child labor laws remained a highly charged topic. But Mrs. Kelley, in her journeys to all parts of the country and in her articles in a wide variety of magazines, persisted in keeping the subject to the fore, in presenting current facts and urging the need for local action in combatting the evil of using child labor in industry. With humor, satire, and exhortation she vitalized issues often dismissed as too technical to interest the general public. Even her printed reports as general secretary of the Consumers League were far from the usual colorless compression of facts. Even the minutiae of child labor regulations became known and gradually awoke response.

Massachusetts was the yardstick by which other states were measured. Mrs. Kelley published the Massachusetts law in full each year and held it up as a standard for other states to move toward. In her report for 1903 she wrote: "On the Pacific Coast, Oregon and Washington have made a long stride, having gone from the group of states with no restrictions into the topmost group which prohibit children from working until they are full fourteen years old."

She claimed nothing for herself in this accomplishment, but merely speculated on "what share the National Consumers League may have had in stimulating this action by bringing to the attention of leaders of thought and action in these two enlightened states, both the anomalous position in which they stood and also the excellence of the Massachusetts statute which they have copied more nearly than any other of the states which have enacted laws during 1903."

But now in 1903, New York had overtaken and in some

respects excelled Massachusetts.[1] Should not the New York
act henceforth be regarded as the standard?

On the other hand, side by side with these gains, there
had been lamentable failure: "The new law of California
appears to be a model of how not to draft a child labor law.
It appears to embody the maximum number possible of
weak points," Mrs. Kelley wrote the same year. (The fourteen-year age limit did not apply if the parent was physi-
cally disabled.) "California thus joins the ranks of the states
which sordidly burden young children with the effort to do
the impossible—to maintain themselves and their disabled
relatives, to carry the responsibilities which more enlightened communities undertake in the care of the sick and the
destitute."

In the East, too, especially in Pennsylvania where she
had been active in the campaign against child labor, the
record was bad. Little boys under fourteen years had finally
been protected from employment in the coal breakers, but
"wretched is the condition, however, of the little girls, who at
the age of thirteen years may be regularly and legally employed twelve hours at night in the textile mills."

Thus she continually played up, by way of contrast, the
adequacy or inadequacy of states or statutes, seeking to
stimulate the laggards by the better performance of their
neighbors. At a time when no other national organization
and no federal agency existed in the United States to combat
child labor, except for sporadic efforts by the trades unions,
Florence Kelley was reiterating to each community she
reached, and to her legion of correspondents, where each
state stood comparatively in the total picture. Her own
passionate concern carried conviction; and while action
often did not follow until long afterward, without her relent-

---

[1] In Massachusetts the maximum working hours were a ten-hour
day, a fifty-four-hour week. In New York the new law had reduced
the maximum to a nine-hour day, a fifty-four-hour week, and included
"nearly all the other good points of the Massachusetts statute."

less reiteration of the facts it might have been much longer delayed.

Mrs. Kelley also played an important role in three other organizations which, in addition to the Consumers League, have perhaps done most to protect American children from industrial exploitation. These were the New York Child Labor Committee founded in 1902, the National Child Labor Committee founded two years later, and the federal Children's Bureau, first proposed in 1906 and established by law in 1912.

THE NEW YORK CHILD LABOR COMMITTEE

In 1902, at the instigation of Mrs. Kelley and Lillian Wald, the New York settlement houses appointed a Child Labor Committee (later separately incorporated), and Robert Hunter, of the University Settlement, was the chairman. He succeeded in collecting a fund sufficient to employ an investigator, Miss Helen Marot. Through Miss Marot and a group of volunteers from the settlements, over a thousand cases of child labor were collected.

It was in connection with this investigation of child labor that my own association with Mrs. Kelley really began. In the fall of 1902, as I recall it, the field work had been completed, and Miss Marot was struggling with the perennial difficulty of organizing a mass of details and reducing it to readable proportions. There were few or no American precedents for such an undertaking. The Massachusetts reports of Carroll Wright and the Illinois reports of Mrs. Kelley stood out in lonely eminence in the American literature. Mrs. Kelley undertook to help Helen Marot write up the findings. In so doing she began that generous aid to younger colleagues in mastering their material which she was to continue all her life. I recall her offering similar assistance in later years in training other investigators-in-the-making who subsequently became well known in their own right. Among them were Mary Van Kleeck, when she held the Collegiate

Alumnae Fellowship for investigating girls' work; Crystal
Eastman, as secretary of the Ives Commission which secured
the first Workmen's Compensation Law in New York; Frances Perkins, Nelle Swartz, and Elinore Herrick as secretaries of the New York Consumers League; Josephine Roche,
Margaret Browne, my sister Pauline, Emily Sims Marconnier, myself, and various others.

I well remember how Mrs. Kelley issued an edict setting
aside Saturday morning as the time for a weekly meeting
of the committee to go over the various sections of Helen
Marot's report. I sat in on those Saturday meetings because
I was working at odd jobs for Mrs. Kelley as a volunteer.
She had then no funds for a paid assistant. She was doing
everything herself: speaking, traveling, inspecting factories,
and typing her own letters.

It was at one of these Saturday morning meetings that
Mrs. Kelley turned to me and handed over a sheaf of papers.
They consisted of questionnaires giving partial histories of
former newsboys confined at the New York Juvenile Asylum
and the Catholic Protectory, two reformatory schools in New
York City. The questionnaires had been filled out by the
"home visitors" of the two institutions. The problem was:
What evidence did they show about the relationship between the boys' work as newsboys and their delinquency?
No previous study of this topic existed. Mrs. Kelley asked
me to check these questionnaires and report what they
showed. I had had no special training for such work, but
neither had any other recent college graduate. In those
days there were no schools of social work,[2] no college
courses on industrial or even civic problems. I had majored
in English at Bryn Mawr, but I had also been brought up
in the tradition of liberal "reform," and I went to work
eagerly on the papers handed over to me by Mrs. Kelley.

I marvel now at my own boldness in traveling Uptown

[2] The New York School of Philanthrophy had been founded in
1898, but in 1902 it had no courses in industrial subjects.

to the New York Juvenile Asylum (later moved to the country and transformed into the Children's Village) to check the boys' histories. I next visited the Catholic Protectory. I was fortunate in this assignment, my first, for the boys proved responsive; and in informal talks with each one I could check and amplify the information—as to age, home conditions, earnings, hours worked, and the like—originally obtained by the home visitors of the institutions. That work as a newsboy in a great city often led to juvenile delinquency became clear enough to be documented. In addition, I had absorbed more than enough background and human interest stories about the boys' experiences to enable me to turn the material into a feature article. This I proceeded to do and, to my joy, the article not only pleased Mrs. Kelley but was accepted and published by the old *New York Evening Post.* This article was the first writing I had ever done for which I received payment. The kindness with which Oswald G. Villard, editor of the *Evening Post,* treated me was a good example of the friendly relations the National Consumers League was to enjoy with the press, for soon after, the League felt the need of a publications secretary and I was appointed.

Over the years, Mrs. Kelley's articles appeared in general magazines, in women's magazines, and in trade union journals. We made it our special business to prepare "raw material" dealing with our legislative and other activities for such diverse editiorial writers as Dr. Lyman Abbott of the *Outlook* and later for Ernest and Lawrence Abbott; for Dr. Hamilton Holt of the *Independent,* for Norman Hapgood of *Collier's* and for *McClure's,* and in later years for the *New Republic* and *The Nation.* As to Mrs. Kelley's influence on the *Survey* and *Survey Graphic* I have already quoted the editor, Paul Kellogg. The old *New York World* was one of our mainstays. The crusading power of its editorial page has, I suppose, rarely been equaled, and we enlisted it to great effect, for instance, in our campaign in the twenties against the terrible death toll from radium poisoning in industry (see Chapter 16).

Mrs. Kelley worked untiringly with the New York Child Labor Committee from its beginning in 1902. She was as regular as the clock in her attendance at meetings of the board of directors, available whenever possible at hearings on child labor bills in Albany, and always in close touch with the executives of the committee, George A. Hall and Jane V. Minor.

An illustration of the pioneer work of the committee which Mrs. Kelley especially valued was its solution of the problem of obtaining "proof of age" of children who wanted to go to work. This may sound like a technical detail in child labor legislation. In fact, it is a foundation stone without which the best standards to protect child workers are meaningless. The most important thing in a child labor law is the minimum age at which children may work. In 1902 in New York the law nominally prohibited the employment of children under fourteen and required work certificates of those between fourteen and sixteen. Such work certificates were granted on the basis of parents' affidavits. Mrs. Kelley had seen in Illinois the readiness of parents to swear to false ages so that their children could go to work below the legal age. In the same way in New York there was a steady stream of eleven-, twelve-, and thirteen-year-old children entering the factories, all armed with false affidavits or certificates based on false affidavits.

In the new law which the New York Child Labor Committee succeeded in putting through the legislature in 1903, parents' affidavits of age were not acceptable. Instead, the health officer who issued the employment certificate was required to obtain from the applicant some documentary proof of age such as a birth certificate, passport, baptismal certificate, or other record showing the date of the child's birth. No other form of evidence was allowed.

Too often a birth certificate could not be obtained because it did not exist. "It is easier," wrote Mrs. Kelley, "to get birth certificates for little Turks born in Turkey than for American children born in the rural counties of New York State." Later Mrs. Kelley enthusiastically supported the long campaign of the U. S. Children's Bureau to induce all states to require birth registration. But what could be done in New York in 1903? The Child Labor Committee was being criticized and the new law attacked because some children could not produce the required documentary proof and hence could not go to work. Many school officials wanted authority to certify children for work in case the required proof was not produced. This the Child Labor Committee opposed, declaring that it would result in practically breaking down the age requirement.

Mrs. Kelley pointed to what the Consumers League was doing in Illinois as a possible solution. Under the Illinois law the county judge issued child labor certificates, and the law permitted him to accept a parent's affidavit if no documentary proof could be obtained. One county judge, seeing how frequently these affidavits were fraudulent, agreed after many conferences to refer to the secretary of the Consumers League all children applying for permits who could not produce documentary proof of age. "In every case," wrote Mrs. Kelley in praise of this work of the Illinois League, "the secretary found it possible through correspondence with various officials either in the United States or abroad to ascertain the real age of the child."

Now the New York Child Labor Committee tried the same method on a much wider scale. With the consent of the New York City Board of Health which issued the "working papers," the committee in 1907 placed its assistant secretary in the Manhattan Board of Health office for the precise purpose of helping children to obtain the requisite evidence of age. For eight years she successfully carried out this assignment.

An amazing variety of papers was turned up which

afforded satisfactory proof of age: naturalization papers, ship's manifests, insurance policies, certificates of circumcision, family Bible entries, court records. For foreign-born children, information was obtained through a State Department letter sent to American consuls abroad and checked by interviews with consuls in New York City. A pamphlet embodying this information, prepared by the New York Committee and published by the National Child Labor Committee, became much in demand throughout the country. Mrs. Kelley took great satisfaction in this achievement which she had done much to bring about, and which she stressed in her addresses throughout the country as an admirable instance of cooperation between public and private agencies.

I must not, however, minimize the difficulties of this accomplishment or the antagonism encountered. Many school officials opposed the new law because it forced them to keep in their schools children they would gladly have dismissed. For, in addition to the better enforcement of the age minimum, the new law provided for a new document—the "school record." Before the health authorities could issue an employment certificate, they had to obtain a record signed by the school principal certifying that the child had completed the required schooling. A minority of school principals fought this simple requirement long and bitterly. Some even certified falsely to get rid of backward children or to enable children to go to work because of poverty at home. The Child Labor Committee opposed exceptions for either of these groups. To permit them to drop out of school was not a real solution in either case. Later, special ungraded classes for retarded children and "scholarships" to help families where children's earnings were especially needed provided ways of dealing constructively with the needs of these children. Mrs. Kelley was especially interested in the scholarship plan which was started by Miss Addams in Chicago after Illinois passed its first enforceable child labor law. Mrs.

Kelley urged this plan in every state she visited, and served for years on the scholarship committee in New York City.

She also worked in many ways to win acceptance of the new requirements—especially by school people. I remember vividly one special occasion when the New York Child Labor Committee had called a meeting to discuss the educational requirements of the law. The room was filled with school officials, public and parochial. Each in turn rose and denounced the Committee for preventing children from earning an honest livelihood. The temperature of the discussion kept rising, inflamed the more by conciliatory explanations of the new law. Paul Kellogg was presiding and tried in vain to stem the tide. The meeting developed into an unrelieved denunciation of the Child Labor Committee and all its works.

All this time Mrs. Kelley was sitting at the back of the room saying nothing, but a bright spot of color burned on each cheek. Finally she arose and walked slowly forward. Her timing was perfect. She turned slowly and faced her audience with a lovely smile. Her voice with its rich inflections fell like music upon that tense and angry silence. "I feel," she began, and a little laugh as spontaneous and disarming as a child's slipped out, "as though I had been living in Alice's Wonderland. The children's best friends, the teachers, have been transformed."

Everyone, pro and con, laughed together. Mrs. Kelley had the meeting completely in hand, and made a plea, which could not be denied, for understanding and a fair trial of the law. The meeting broke up, if not in agreement, at least in tolerance.

THE NATIONAL CHILD LABOR COMMITTEE

I have told the early New York story in detail because Mrs. Kelley set great store by the pioneer work of the New York Child Labor Committee, and because it illustrates her dynamic influence on any board on which she served.

However, the major fight on child labor was naturally not in New York but in those states in which industrial development was newest and employment least regulated; that is, in the South.

In her annual report for 1903, Mrs. Kelley noted among the legislative accomplishments of the year some meager gains on behalf of young children employed in four southern states: Alabama, North and South Carolina, and Arkansas. True, the age limits for beginning work were still as low as ten and twelve years, but even those statutes Mrs. Kelley was willing to record as "valuable and significant" indications of a new public sentiment stirring in these states.

But a few years later, indignant at their continued opposition, she engaged in a violent controversy with mill-owner apologists and defenders of child labor in the South. Thus, in 1907, her fighting spirit was aroused by a letter published in *Outlook* by Mr. Elison A. Smyth, of Pelzer, South Carolina (a cotton manufacturer of twenty-six years' experience) protesting against criticism of the South. Mrs. Kelley replied in a blast against what she termed *"Six Black List States."*

Alabama, Florida, Georgia, Mississippi, South Carolina and Texas have no State Department of Labor . . . no State Factory Inspector, no compulsory education law, and therefore no truant officers or comprehensive school enrollment . . . . In the absence of current data, such as would be at hand if all these departments of the state were regularly publishing results of their labors, the public will doubtless fix a critical eye upon estimates furnished by an advocate speaking from within a corporation which employs children under fourteen years of age. . . .

There is one way in which the Southern States can silence the adverse criticism of the civilized world in the matter of child labor. That is by adopting the same methods of dealing with it which the civilized world has successfully adopted. . . . Until these things are done by *all* the Southern States, the investing and purchasing public may be counted upon to continue in no uncertain tone the criticism to which Mr. Smyth so strongly objects, and to give the preference increasingly to goods made under more humane and enlightened conditions.[3]

Against such employers and the dominant practice of employing young children, a courageous southerner, Edgar Gardner Murphy, had started to battle as early as 1901. Murphy was a liberal young Episcopal minister in Montgomery, Alabama, who later resigned from the church to become executive secretary of the Southern Education Board.

A bill to prohibit the employment of young children had been introduced into the Alabama Legislature in November, 1900, but had failed. During that winter the matter had come before the Women's Clubs of Birmingham and the state Women's Christian Temperance Union, but no active campaign resulted.

What was primarily needed were facts as to the actual employment of children in the mills. These facts were obtained when the American Federation of Labor sent Irene Ashby that year to make an investigation of Alabama textile mills. She brought to Mr. Murphy her findings about the children employed in Montgomery. He was surprised and shocked by the conditions she had found in the mills, and thereafter he was permanently enlisted in the struggle against child labor, first in Alabama, later throughout the nation.

When a second bill introduced in the Alabama Legislature in 1901 was defeated, the Alabama Child Labor Committee was formed. Murphy took the lead in a campaign of education, writing and editing a series of pamphlets, newspaper articles, and editorials directed against current ignorance or misstatements. The number distributed ran up to 30,000. The first of these pamphlets was entitled *An Appeal to the People and Press of New England*. In Mr. Murphy's words: "Although the citizens of New England might not

[3] Report of the National Consumers League, 1907, pp. 26-28.

know it, the most aggressive and effective opposition [before the legislature] came from the salaried representatives of Massachusetts investments." He appealed against "the heartless policy with which her capital is using and is striving to perpetuate the defenselessness of the children of the South."

Mr. Murphy did not, however, shirk local responsibility. To the plea that action in Alabama should be deferred until neighboring states acted, he dryly rejoined that "over in Georgia and the Carolinas, some of the mill-men are claiming that they are only waiting upon Alabama."

Two years later, in 1903, a compromise measure was passed. The compromise was reluctantly accepted by the Alabama Child Labor Committee and the Alabama Federation of Women's Clubs in conferences with the manufacturers. It was a small gain but at least the battle had been joined.[4]

In this battle Florence Kelley had played a part, indirect but unmistakable. In June, 1900, the General Federation of Women's Clubs at its biennial meeting in Milwaukee had devoted one of its sessions to the Consumers League. Mrs. Kelley spoke and stressed particularly the need of combatting child labor. The response to this meeting, wrote Mrs. Kelley the next winter, was "still perceptible at our office in the form of invitations for speakers, requests for literature, and a vast increase in correspondence." What she valued most was her appointment as chairman of a committee of the General Federation on industrial problems affecting women and children.

The women's clubs of the period had mostly busied themselves with literary and cultural subjects. Florence Kelley offered them a more Spartan diet. To the state federations, and local clubs of the General Federation, she sent a circular pointing out the industrial issues at stake for in-

_____
[4] The new law provided a twelve-year age limit, a sixty-six-hour week and exemption of children of ten years "to support a dependent parent."

telligent women who had "a vast power to contribute at once, toward a peaceful and beneficent solution." She asked the clubs to devote programs to the three-fold aspect of the subject: women in the home, women as purchasers, women and children as employees. Under each heading she presented lists of collateral reading, and she asked bluntly for answers to four concrete questions: "What is the legal age for employing children in your state? Have you a woman factory inspector? Is there a license law for manufacture in homes? What is the legal working day?"

Fifty years ago, such a communication was not buried under an avalanche of appeals and printed matter as it would be today; and the appeal itself fell upon ears not yet inured to global misery and cries for relief. The club women in Alabama as in other states were, it is true, often the wives or relatives of textile manufacturers. It took courage for them to oppose the prevalent system of child labor. Yet the blunt appeal of the General Federation's own committee on industry, followed by vigorous correspondence, undoubtedly helped to stimulate women in the clubs to join local efforts to stem the tide of youthful, even infantile, recruits to the mills. So it proved in Alabama; the president of the Alabama Federation of Women's Clubs was spokesman for her group in negotiations for the compromise child labor law of 1903.

Murphy followed up his initial work in his own state by a powerful address on child labor as a national issue at the National Conference of Charities and Corrections at Atlanta in 1903.[5] This reinforcement from within the Deep South was enthusiastically received by such earlier workers against child labor as Jane Addams and Florence Kelley, and by a young newspaper man, A. J. McKelway, who later became the effective southern secretary of the National Child Labor Committee.

Meantime it was becoming evident to the various state

---

[5] The name of the organization was changed in 1915 to National Conference of Social Work.

groups seeking to check the premature employment of children that a broader attack upon this widespread evil was needed. The New York City Child Labor Committee took the initiative in appointing a committee consisting of Felix Adler, William H. Baldwin, and Florence Kelley to draft a proposal for a national child labor organization. This committee consulted at length with Mr. Murphy, who had indeed proposed such an organization and whose new work on the Southern Education Board brought him frequently to New York. Aided by his intimate acquaintance with southerners in sympathy with the project, the National Child Labor Committee was launched with about thirty members. A board of trustees directed the work, and of these a third were from the South. Obviously the enlistment of southern support was a first requisite for a movement which would inevitably arouse more hostility in the stronghold of child labor than in communities already committed to improved standards.

With Samuel McCune Lindsay, the first secretary, and Owen D. Lovejoy, assistant secretary of the new National Child Labor Committee, Florence Kelley was well acquainted. Her office was in the same building as theirs, and she was what might be called a "working member" of the board of trustees, in constant touch with the development of the work.[6] She was thus for years a spokesman both for her own organization and for the new committee. The special project on which the latter group embarked in 1906 enlisted for life her enthusiastic participation. This was the establishment of a Children's Bureau in the federal government and its support year in and year out.

---

[6] At a later period, Mrs. Kelley broke with the National Child Labor Committee over the federal child labor law of 1916.

Chapter **8**

Julia Lathrop and the Children's Bureau

In no phase of Florence Kelley's life is the impact of her private life and temperament upon her public work more evident than in her passionate championship of the U. S. Children's Bureau. While this was but one of her many-sided activities—indeed only one facet of her work for children—it was for years emotionally predominating.

The black shadow cast upon her mother's life by the death of five little daughters had clouded Florence Kelley's youth and remained ineradicable. She would be "false to the memory of a tender and grief-stricken mother," she wrote at the height of the conflict over the first federal-state maternity program, if she did not combat, by every means in her power, these largely avoidable and preventable tragedies. Her deepest instinct, as I have already emphasized, was maternal; in the conception, creation, and long defense of the Children's Bureau, that instinct found a natural outlet. "Of all the activities in which I have shared during more than forty years of striving," she wrote of one of the major activities of the Bureau, "none is, I am convinced, of such fundamental importance as the Sheppard-Towner Act."

In her work with the Children's Bureau Mrs. Kelley was associated with its first chief, Julia Lathrop, who had been one of her closest friends in the old days at Hull House.

Something of a legend has developed about the Children's Bureau, its origin, its scope, and its survival under attack. It has to its credit concrete achievements in which, at various stages, Florence Kelley was deeply involved and which are thus necessarily a part of the history of her life. Beyond its concrete accomplishments, the Bureau has demonstrated over the years the power of a great idea.

Here was an organ of the federal government, minute in size compared to the large departments, minute for years in its appropriations, but built upon a genuinely great conception: that a child cannot be divided into parts; hence all the government services for children should be integrated in one agency. Against the Bureau, from time to time, have been arrayed forces determined to control or subordinate it. But somehow, at each crisis of its existence, the power of that basic conception of conserving childhood in its totality had so seized upon the imagination of the country, in particular had so gained a hold upon the women of the country, that the most powerful opposition retired before it.[1]

To Lillian Wald has rightly been ascribed the first suggestion of a federal Children's Bureau. Florence Kelley, like everyone else, always referred to her as the "author" of the idea. Evidence exists, however, to show the joint responsibility of the two friends for this far-reaching conception. As early as the summer of 1900, Mrs. Kelley lectured on the subject of child labor. In a series of addresses repeated at various universities and colleges, she broke new ground in proposing what she called a National Commission for Children, which should do for all phases of child life what the U. S. Department of Agriculture did for life on the farm; that is, "To make available and interpret the facts concern-

---

[1] Under the Reorganization Act of 1946, the Children's Bureau was removed from the Labor Department and placed under the Federal Security Agency. It was transferred as a unit except for the Industrial Division which was kept in the Labor Department where it continues to administer the industrial work for children.

ing the physical, mental, and moral conditions and prospects of the children of the United States."

In her book, *Some Ethical Gains Through Legislation,* Mrs. Kelley incorporated the substance of these earlier lectures and outlined the "probable field of work" of her proposed commission for children.[2] There were within the federal government, she pointed out, three bureaus (Education, Labor, and the Census) charged with the study of certain separate phases of child life. But there was no single central agency devoted to *all* the interests of the children. Therefore, in her opinion, "the facts gathered by the three above-named departments remain uncorrelated and largely unused." The problems of children were to her mind "interrelated in such complex ways that it is very difficult to state them in logical order." She suggested seven subjects of immediate urgency: infant mortality, birth registration, orphanage, child labor, desertion, illegitimacy, degeneracy.

The arguments later advanced on these specific topics during six years of hearings and Congressional debates over creation of the Children's Bureau were all foreshadowed in Mrs. Kelley's long-forgotten little book. For instance, as to infant mortality, she made a point later elaborated repeatedly on the floor of Congress.

If lobsters or young salmon become scarce or are in danger of perishing, the United States Fish Commission takes active steps in the matter. But infant mortality continues excessive, from generation to generation, in perfectly well-defined areas; yet no one organ of the national government is interested in the matter sufficiently even to gather, collate and publish consecutive information about this social phenomenon. . . . More constructive criticism from an authoritative source, consecutively afforded by the proposed commission, could not fail to have a stimulating effect upon local officials.[3]

---

[2] *Some Ethical Gains Through Legislation* (New York, 1905), p. 99.

[3] *Some Ethical Gains Through Legislation* (New York, 1905), p. 101.

"In Mrs. Kelley's book published in 1905, we find a plan for a United States Commission for Children whose scope and purpose was carried out in concise form in the Children's Bureau Act of 1912," wrote Julia Lathrop in an obituary of Mrs. Kelley.[4]

As early as 1903, Lillian Wald's quick imagination produced the idea of a separate bureau for children, to be established in one of the federal departments, which should do for them what Mrs. Kelley had proposed for a national commission; that is, set standards of care in all fields, based on scientific study. This proposal was soon conveyed by Mrs. Kelley to Edward T. Devine, their common friend and fellow trustee of the National Child Labor Committee, editor of the little sheet known as *Charities*, later *Survey Graphic*. On September 19, 1903, Mr. Devine wrote to Miss Wald, asking: "Is not the first step to get the plan and some evidence of need of it into print? Would you be willing to write out a statement for *Charities?* If so, I am quite willing to give considerable attention to it, subsequently getting others to write upon it."

Mr. Devine also sent word of Miss Wald's proposal to President Theodore Roosevelt. An invitation was promptly received from the White House to come to Washington and tell the President more about the idea. In a hearing before a House Committee, later, Miss Wald described that initial interview. "It was a coincidence," said Miss Wald in her testimony, "that the Secretary of Agriculture was departing that same morning to the South, to find out what danger to the community lurked in the appearance of the boll weevil. That brought home with a very strong emphasis the fact that nothing that could have happened to the children would have called forth such official action on the part of the government." [5]

---

[4] Quoted in Jane Addams' *My Friend, Julia Lathrop* (New York, 1935), p. 130.

[5] 60th Congress, 2d session. *House Hearings*, January 27, 1909, p. 34.

Two years (1904-06) were devoted by the National Child Labor Committee to the business of drafting a bill for the proposed bureau and marshaling support for it among important individuals and the many agencies working with children throughout the nation. The three departments of the government dealing with separate phases of child life, the Bureau of Education, the Bureau of the Census, and the Bureau of Labor were consulted at length. Two letters written nearly a quarter-century later show the importance of Mrs. Kelley and Miss Wald in the drafting of the bill. Julia Lathrop, first chief of the Bureau, wrote to Mrs. Kelley in 1930 to learn who had proposed the paragraph in the bill authorizing the Bureau to investigate *all* phases of child life as well as specific enumerated problems. "I am very eager," she wrote, "to show the place of scientific research in government, especially in the new social field, and to show the vast astuteness and foresight of those of you who worked for the bill. Anything as to how that comprehensive paragraph was obtained . . . I would like to know."

Mrs. Kelley replied:

Last evening I dined at Miss Wald's and their filing clerk fished out a mass of Congressional reports, bills, newspaper clippings, reprints of articles about the campaign from 1909 through 1912 which then culminated in the creation of the Bureau and your appointment. Pertinent samples of these Miss Wald promised to mail to you this morning. I do not know where to look for anything comparable to that collection. She and I really concocted that phrase about the length, breadth, and thickness of the duties of the Children's Bureau. I remember haggling with her about putting illegitimacy into that itemized list. At that time the itemized list seemed to me far more important than the generalized authorization "to investigate everything appertaining to. . . ." How different experience has shown the case to be.

The second annual meeting of the National Child Labor Committee was held in Washington, D.C., in December, 1905. An incident which occurred there is worth recounting as an example of the conflict of opposites in Florence Kelley's nature—her mature, dynamic, articulate intelligence and the excessive impulsiveness to which she would at times yield, to her own subsequent chagrin.

At the evening meeting Mrs. Kelley was one of the principal speakers, her topic, "The Federal Government and the Working Children." It was a great speech, direct and impassioned, a plea for research and information about "all the children in the republic." The child-employing textile industry, she pointed out, extended from North to South; at that very moment the great glass industry in at least eight states was employing little boys all night,[6] and in only two of them, Ohio and Illinois, was there even a pretense of prohibiting such employment by law.

The federal bureaus charged with investigating separate phases of child life published information so inconclusive and belated that it was worthless as a basis for action by the states. It was the laughing stock of Europeans interested in our institutions. A "feeble volunteer society" (referring to the National Consumers League) was left to "collect a few hundred dollars here and there and publish in January every year the new statutes which have taken effect in the twelve months next preceding."[7] No federal agency performed even this elementary service. She reiterated her old plea, the need for trustworthy facts: "It is proposed that there should be devoted to the children one bureau of our government, by means of which the people should be able to obtain from month to month, recent trustworthy information concerning everything that enters into the lives of the children; everything that makes for or against their vital effi-

---

[6] New York, Pennsylvania, Delaware, West Virginia, Ohio, Indiana, Illinois, and Missouri.

[7] In 1902 a summary of child labor legislation had been prepared for the General Federation of Women's Clubs by Madeline Wallin Sykes. In 1903 the League took over this task, enlarging the summary into a handbook which, as publications secretary, I compiled for six years thereafter.

ciency, their educational opportunity, their future industrial and civic value."

Mrs. Kelley ended with a solemn indictment of the three existing federal bureaus: "The hieroglyphics on the pyramid of Cheops are not more remote from the life of today than their statistics are remote from the life of the working children of Georgia and Pennsylvania."

I remember how Dr. Felix Adler, chairman of the National Child Labor Committee, described the effect of that speech. "She spoke in a solemn monotone, like an antique Sibyl, like a prophetess," he exclaimed. "It cast a spell over the audience. I felt that Mrs. Kelley must be our spokesman, the country over."

But at the same time he told me the story of how she jeopardized the meeting with President Theodore Roosevelt the next day. An appointment had been made for the committee to meet the President to ask his endorsement of the bill about to be introduced in Congress. The committee waited while the President chatted with another group in the same room.

Mrs. Kelley basically distrusted Mr. Roosevelt. She thoroughly condemned his policy of the "Big Stick." She never forgave his actions in seizing Panama. On this occasion she became deeply incensed by the President's loud and jocose remarks to the other group in the room, publicly ridiculing —as it seemed—his wife and her church connections. To the dismay of her fellow delegates, Mrs. Kelley turned abruptly and left the room. No sooner had she allowed herself to act upon this impulse than she realized her folly, "spending an agonized hour at the hotel," in Paul Kellogg's words, before she learned that she had not thereby imperiled the bill.

Six years elapsed before the bill was passed. It took three years of agitation and publicity before even the first hearings were held. Opposition centered on two main issues, reiterated for years: that the new bureau would merely duplicate work for children already performed by the other bureaus and that it would invade both parental and states' rights.

The proponents of the measure spared no pains in defending their case in protracted hearings. Their position was powerfully reinforced by the first White House Conference on the Care of Dependent Children, called in 1909. Acting upon a resolution of the conference, President Roosevelt sent a special message to Congress urging enactment of the Children's Bureau bill.[8] But it was not until 1912, after protracted hearings, letters, publicity, and long debates on the floor of Senate and House, that the bill was passed. So determined was the opposition in Congress that before its final vote the Senate devoted five days to debating the issue. In the final struggle the child labor argument was brought out into the open. Senator Reed of Missouri spoke bluntly, "Why is this bill opposed. . .? Why is this oppositon coming from Senators who represent states that have cotton mills in them? Is it because there are unspeakable conditions in those mills? I think the main objection to the bill, from some sources at least, lies in the fact that information on that subject is what is not desired by the proprietors of those institutions." [9]

Similar charges were made in the House. Despite this opposition, the bill was finally enacted and signed by President Taft on April 12, 1912.

With Julia Lathrop as its head, Florence Kelley felt from the first a sense of personal identification with this new agency for children. In Illinois her efforts on behalf of the glass house boys, the little victims of the sweatshops, and other working children had been frustrated by politics. Her own organization, the Consumers League, and other volunteer bodies were naturally limited in scope and in funds.

[8] In later years, Florence Kelley bitterly compared this initial presidential support and the backing of the second White House Conference of 1919 under President Wilson, with the destructive tactics of the third White House Conference of 1930 under President Hoover.

[9] *Congressional Record,* Vol. 42, Part 2, p. 1571. 62d Congress, 2d session.

Now, under the aegis of the federal government, what might not be accomplished in basic research and nation-wide stimulus? The future was exciting, yet sobering in its responsibility. No false moves must endanger a prospect so fair, so promising.

The purpose of the Bureau, Miss Lathrop declared, was "to serve all children, to try to work out the standards of care and protection which shall give to every child his fair chance in the world." With an initial appropriation of $25,000 and a staff of fifteen persons, where in this vast field should she begin? The Bureau must among other things establish a reputation for scientific disinterestedness and accuracy. It must try to avoid controversy to keep and gain support in Congress for the sake of its annual appropriation. What should it do first? Miss Lathrop took counsel with those responsible for the creation of the Bureau—among them, naturally, Florence Kelley. Mrs. Kelley was ready with her answer. As she wrote later: "When the Children's Bureau bill passed in 1912, I was consulted among its advocates as to the order in which the subjects assigned for inquiry should be taken up. I urged immediate study of infant mortality. Sir Arthur Newsholm's monumental volume, then recent, pointed the way and revealed by contrast this Republic's deplorable ignorance concerning our young children." [10]

What was the infant death rate in the United States? Nobody knew. Everyone knew about babies' 'summer complaint,' as it was then called, which carried off the very young in appalling numbers. But we could not know the death rate of babies, because we did not even know the birth rate. As late as 1911 the Bureau of the Census regarded registration of births fairly complete only in the New England states, Pennsylvania, and Michigan. To stimulate birth registration in all the states became an early Children's Bureau enterprise.

---

[10] *Survey Graphic,* October 1, 1926, p. 8.

"Baby-Saving Campaigns" was the disarming title of Julia Lathrop's first report. This could scarcely be resented by the most rabid opponent of a federal agency for children. It was a slender pamphlet giving the replies to an inquiry sent by the Bureau to the 109 cities of the United States with a population of 50,000 or more, inquiring of the measures taken for the summer care of babies.

The next publication about infant mortality was called: "The New Zealand Society for the Health of Women and Children. An Example of Methods of Baby-Saving Work in Small Towns and Rural Districts."

Why should the new Bureau report on this remote Pacific country? Because it was recognized to have the lowest infant death rate in the world, 51 per thousand. While the death rate for the United States as a whole was unknown, "estimates tend to show," wrote Miss Lathrop, "that it is at least twice the rate in New Zealand."

After these initial reports the Bureau started on the first systematic inquiries into the death rate of American babies. Eight cities and rural districts were covered. Again Miss Lathrop's methods were disarming. They were also totally new. Field investigations covered the economic, social, and civic factors surrounding the lives of all children born within a given year. In each area studied, the history of every baby born was traced from birth through the first twelve months of life, or as long as the baby lived in that first year.

Everyone who read those early reports when they came out will remember the shock of their impact. We had taken for granted American superiority in sanitation and health. American plumbing was the sign and symbol, the world over, of our national pre-eminence in physical care. Now for the first time, in this house-to-house canvass, was disclosed a very different and horrifying state of affairs. Babies under one year were dying at a rate unthought of: for the United States as a whole, a quarter of a million babies were dying each year. The maternal death rate was also shocking, higher than the deaths of women from any other cause except tuberculosis, higher than that in any other civilized country of the world. The infant and maternal death rates were intimately connected. In Waterbury, Connecticut, the Bureau found the infant death rate was three times greater among the babies whose mothers died than among those whose mothers lived; in Baltimore, it was five times greater.[11]

To Florence Kelley such figures could never be cold statistics. From childhood she had been conditioned to see behind them the heartbreak she had known in her parental home. She seized every opportunity to aid in giving wide publicity to the findings of the Bureau. For instance, she wrote:

These earliest studies showed that six nations were more successful than we in keeping their babies alive to the first birthday; that our maternal death rate was the highest among civilized nations which kept records; and that a baby's chance of living was six times as good if its mother lived and could stay at home with it during its early weeks, as when she had to go back to the factory or do heavy work at home.[12]

These facts were properly the concern of the Consumers League, organized to improve the lot of working people, Mrs. Kelley said.

This activity is a part of the League's thirty years' long striving to interest and inform the indifferent consuming public as to its own share of responsibility for conditions in industry. The infant mortality studies having early demonstrated the excessive

[11] "The Bureau therefore began the collection and interpretation of statistics of maternal mortality, including a careful study of every maternal death in thirteen states, occurring over a two-year period, and in two states over a one-year period, about 7500 deaths in all. The recommendations drafted by the Children's Bureau's advisory committee on obstetrics, based on the findings of these studies, provided for leadership and the setting of standards for maternal care by the medical profession, and for strengthening the education of the general public in regard to the need for and meaning of adequate maternal care." U. S. Department of Labor, *History and Functions of the Children's Bureau*, September 1, 1944, p. 6.

[12] *The Nation*, April 23, 1930, p. 481.

death rates of mothers and babies in the working population, our interest was permanently enlisted. A workingman's family of little children newly bereft of their mother is a scene of desolation. The father's job is imperilled if he tries to shift for himself and them. Often the children have to be separated and distributed among relatives or placed in institutions. Then the family disintegrates.[13]

What was to be done? A considerable body of facts had been disclosed. They were impressive, even shocking. They called for dynamic action.

[13] Statement submitted by Mrs. Kelley to the Senate Committee on Commerce on S. 255, 1929.

Chapter **9**

Federal Help for Mothers and Babies

In her annual report for 1917, Miss Lathrop put forward officially for the first time in this country a plan for the "public protection of maternity and infancy." In this proposal she followed the precedent set by federal aid extended to the states for agriculture, for vocational training, for good roads. She proposed the extension of local maternal and child health services through grants of federal funds to be administered by state health agencies. Standards of administration of such local services were to be set by the Bureau. More public health nurses, medical examination and advice for well children, adequate confinement care and hospital facilities were some of the items in her program.

"Millions will be necessary from the federal government to be matched by millions from the states," she wrote in a later amplification of her plan. "Will such expenditures be questioned?" She cited the example of England where in August, 1918, Parliament had passed a law providing grants-in-aid to be used for purposes analogous to those she had outlined. Such protection, well justified by results, was already in effect in New Zealand. It was being considered in Australia.

The infant and maternity bill urged by the Children's Bureau was introduced in 1918. After three years of agitation and debate it became a law in 1921, popularly known as the Sheppard-Towner Act. A direct outgrowth of the Bureau's studies of infant and maternal mortality, it followed the lines proposed in Miss Lathrop's initial proposal, the first measure to appropriate federal funds for a social welfare purpose. For seven years it demonstrated successful federal-state cooperation in a social welfare project. In 1929 it failed to secure further appropriations from Congress, but six years later it was renewed on a much more ambitious scale as part of the Social Security Act of 1935.

During the agitation for the maternity bill and its seven years of operation with the annual struggle for its appropriation, Mrs. Kelley was in the forefront of the battle. She spent herself as though aid to mothers and babies had sole claim upon her time, her sympathies, and her philosophy.

Perhaps the highwater mark of her eloquence and power of persuasion was reached at a Senate hearing on December 20, 1920. Those who heard her that day could never forget the effect of her quiet words, the tension which underlay her measured voice and gripped her audience.

The Consumers League endorsed this measure, she said, because the League was concerned primarily with the industrial life of women and children, because of "the terrible death rates of mothers and children where the mothers work in factories and workshops until the time of the birth of the child. According to the best information available, the children under one year are dying at the rate of a quarter of a million a year."

It was Christmas week when people's minds turn especially, she reminded them, to thoughts of children. People would soon go to church on Christmas and remember not only the Child who was born on that day but also the circumstances under which that Child was born. The story of Herod would be remembered. "We do not know," she said, "how many children were slaughtered by the order of Herod; history does not record that. But the deaths of those children have remained in the minds of the human race for nearly two thousand years."

Now she was haunted by the thought of those quarter of a million American children who would die this year; dying for the most part unnecessarily, for lack of care for babies and mothers. Although history did not record the number of children slaughtered by the order of Herod, the Congress, she said, "has to choose where it will be recorded in history . . . after its long delay and its failure to interest itself in these daily deaths of 680 children—or 20,000 a month."

She paused in a tense silence and continued:

If by some fearful catastrophe, the Senate of the United States had been obliterated in a day, for instance—if that had happened any day last week— the entire world would today have been condoling with the United States over our frightful loss. But every day since this bill was introduced—two years ago—six times as many children on an average have died every day, on Sundays and holidays, and Christmas day, every day, as there are men in the United States Senate.

Still in measured tones, she then launched the peroration that became famous:

But when we are told that this country is so poor and this Congress so harassed by things of greater importance than the deaths of a quarter of a million children a year, we say to ourselves, "surely, we are not to take this seriously." Is this really what Congress believes? Is this the way Congress is really going to act? . . . Will Congress let Christmas come and go and New Year's come and go, and the legislatures come, and seven of them adjourn after thirty days, and half of them after sixty days, without being encouraged by Congress to take action for saving the lives of children? Will Congress allow another biennial period to pass? . . . What answer can be given to the women who are marveling and asking "why does Congress wish women and children to die?"

It was true the women of the country (who obtained the suffrage in 1920) were making the maternity bill their first concerted demand. Twelve women's organizations were

ranged behind it. Congressman Cooper of Wisconsin declared that practically every women's organization in the
country, regardless of party, race, or creed was enlisted in
support of the bill.

To be sure, there was some opposition. The National
Association Opposed to Woman Suffrage—not then entirely
defunct—opposed the Sheppard-Towner bill. So did certain
red-baiting groups, the Woman Patriots, and the Sentinels
of the Republic. "Russian," "socialistic" and "bolshevistic"
were epithets hurled against it. Mrs. Kelley, having been
married to a Russian, was obviously the head of an anti-
American conspiracy. The Children's Bureau had included
Russia in one of its pamphlets surveying wartime experience;
this proved that the Bureau was preparing to "nationalize"
American children.

There was other opposition to the Sheppard-Towner bill.
In 1921 it was opposed for the first time by some sections
of the medical profession. The bugaboo of "state medicine"
and interference with private practice was invoked against
the proposal. For the first time, too, the claim was made that
child health work belonged with other health work in the
U. S. Public Health Service. This claim, of course, conflicted
with the basic principle of the Children's Bureau that no
single aspect of child care could be handled alone. The
validity of this principle had been demonstrated by the
Bureau's pioneer studies of infant and maternal mortality
which furnished, on the basis of careful research, graphic
proof that a baby's chances of life or death rested not only
on medical knowledge but rose and fell with the father's
earnings, the mother's instruction in baby care, etc. Fortunately, the opposition did not prevail.

The Children's Bureau in its ten years of existence had
laid the groundwork for the federal-state infant and maternity care program it was now to initiate. By 1922 it had
persuaded forty-six states to set up child hygiene or child
welfare divisions. There was none when the Bureau started

its work. These were the agencies which were to administer the jointly financed standards to be set by the medical division of the Bureau. Already distinguished obstetricians and pediatricians were serving on its advisory boards. The pamphlet entitled *Infant Care* was a "best seller" among government bulletins (ultimately it reached a distribution of twenty million copies).

The Children's Bureau had also cooperated successfully with the states in securing accurate birth registration. When the Bureau was established, only a handful of states did anything effective in this field. Mrs. Kelley worked closely with the Bureau on this project and enlisted the help of women's clubs all over the country. Birth registration was one of the technical subjects she made intelligible, even dramatic. She secured hundreds of club women in a score of states as volunteers to test birth registration methods. By 1921, twenty-seven states were registering all births.

With its approach to health as part of the whole child-welfare problem and its experience in federal-state cooperation, the Children's Bureau was ideally fitted to administer the Sheppard-Towner Act. Under Julia Lathrop's successor, Grace Abbott (also from Hull House), the Bureau carried out this pioneer program with great success. Mrs. Kelley, who continued as unofficial advisor and staunch defender of the Bureau under its new head, wrote of this work in 1926:

For four years this life-saving measure has been administered with extraordinary intelligence and success by the Children's Bureau cooperating with the state health departments. Under its stimulus, public health nurses have been introduced in hundreds of counties where they had hardly been heard of. Clinics and classes for mothers and little children have been spread over backward states, many of which, four years ago, had appallingly high death rates.

State boards of health publish with pride the falling infant death rates and stir in turn the professional pride of local officials and voluntary associations, in this beneficent rivalry.

Lonely ranchers in Arizona and Idaho and slum dwellers in the most congested cities are increasingly able to command resources for safety of their young children, undreamed of by women of my mother's generation. Forty-three states and Hawaii are cooperating—all the states except Connecticut, Illinois, Kansas, Maine and Massachusetts.

My own modest share in this life-saving measure is an abiding happy memory.[1]

The Sheppard-Towner Act was originally passed for a five-year period, but in 1927 it was extended for two additional years. As the end of that period drew near, opposition intensified. It was said that the states should now take over full responsibility. Mrs. Kelley believed that President Hoover was directly responsible for failure to extend the act. Five presidents preceding him, she reminded the country, had in turn actively supported the Children's Bureau. She charged that President Hoover himself requested that the infant and maternity work of the Bureau be ended by denying further appropriations pending the third White House Conference on Children which was to take place in 1930. Committees to prepare for the conference were set up late in 1929. The surgeon general of the Public Health Service, Hugh Cummings, was chairman of the Committee on Public Health Service and Administration. A subcommittee, of which Grace Abbott was a member, recommended, with Miss Abbott dissenting, that all federal health work for children be transferred to the U. S. Public Health Service.

When the conference assembled in November, 1930, "its dominant interest for the press and the public," as Mrs. Kelley reported the story, "was the unforeseen and overwhelming protest of delegates, including many distinguished men and women, against the proposal—that the medical work of the Children's Bureau be transferred to the federal Health Service. This recommendation split the conference beyond all possible reunion."

---

[1] *Survey Graphic,* October 1, 1926, p. 8.

Anyone who attended the two meetings of the conference devoted to the subject remembers the tension of the
atmosphere. The first of these meetings was the one at
which the medical subcommittee presented its report—the
majority statement and Grace Abbott's dissent. A small room
had been assigned for the meeting. It proved entirely inadequate to hold the delegates who crowded in to hear the
report and register their opinions. I recall the array of distinguished people who jammed the room—Lillian Wald and
Florence Kelley from New York, Sophonisba Breckinridge
and Edith Abbott from Chicago, Dorothy Kirchway Brown
from Boston, and many others of eminence in their own
communities.

It was apparent at this meeting that the delegates from
all over the country knew and cared about the work of the
Children's Bureau in the medical field. They had listened to
Julia Lathrop, Grace Abbott, and Florence Kelley, who had
traveled widely for years explaining what the Bureau was
trying to do and why different kinds of work for children
could best be done by a single agency. The medical subcommittee was amazed. It had expected adoption without
much debate of its majority proposal to transfer federal
health work for children to the Public Health Service. After
all, this proposal had the support of the Administration and
presumably of the medical profession. But the delegates to
the conference had other views. Women from all parts of the
country understood the issue and knew what they wanted.
They were powerfully reinforced by telegrams from distinguished doctors, both pediatricians and obstetricians.

Dr. Alice Hamilton (one of the old Hull House group
of Mrs. Kelley's Chicago days) was among the medical
group who opposed the transfer. Said Dr. Hamilton,

The sole argument for the recommendation advanced by its
defendants is that it is *logical* to have all medical work done by
the government headed by medical men. But our government
has never rested on logic. We are pragmatic. What works well

we keep; what proves worthless, we drop. If there were any logic in the organization of our government, how could the U.S. Public Health Service be under the Treasury?

Twelve national organizations of women were represented at the meeting in opposition to the transfer. The proposal to terminate the infant and maternity program of the Children's Bureau met a dead wall of dissent.

Again the next day, in the huge auditorium of Constitution Hall where a final vote was to be taken, the same phenomenon occurred. So the White House Conference adjourned without recommending the transfer of medical work for children to the Public Health Service, and the Children's Bureau continued its research and education work on maternity and infancy.

But the services which had been carried out with Sheppard-Towner funds were abandoned in many states when the federal money lapsed. This was the depth of the depression and it was impossible to secure increased state appropriations for such work. As the health officer of Kentucky declared, speaking for the states which had failed to continue the program, "I cite my own state as an example. Our people historically have been self-dependent, independent, hard working people. But now their farms are ruined by the drought in two successive summers. Their crops are nothing. They are starving. They need food and clothes and shoes. Our banks are closed. It is idle to ask them to pay increased taxes for any new purpose." By February, 1931, only nineteen states had appropriated enough additional money for infant and maternity work to replace the lost federal funds.

Thus the first federal-state infant maternity program for which Mrs. Kelley had worked so hard came to an end. But, as in many another campaign, though the battle was lost, the war was won. For the Children's Bureau remained intact to enter upon its greater role when the time came. When the

Social Security Act was passed in 1935, the Children's Bureau was entrusted with the administration of federal-state services to mothers and children involving annual federal appropriations of some six million dollars in grants to the states. During World War II it administered, again through state agencies, the vast emergency program of infant and maternity care for the wives of servicemen. In 1945 alone, over forty-five million dollars was expended in this program. In November, 1946, the Bureau announced the birth of the millionth baby born under the plan.

Chapter 10

The Fight for a Federal Child Labor Law

"The people of the United States do not wish to use the products of child labor." From the beginning of her work with the Consumers League, Mrs. Kelley preached this gospel in all her journeys up and down the land. In every way she could she encouraged state action to raise child labor standards. Each legislative year she noted with enthusiasm the gains made in one state or another.

But state-by-state progress toward achieving the fourteen-year age minimum for employment was coming too slowly to suit Mrs. Kelley. She soon decided that a national child labor law was indispensable. However, in the years while the bill to create the Children's Bureau was pending, she had taken no part in pressing for such a law, to avoid antagonizing Congressmen and Senators who might vote for creating the Bureau but not for a national child labor law. Opposition to such national action was not confined to those who wanted no interference with existing employment with children. Many people who were working to strengthen state child labor regulation were opposed to a federal law, believing sincerely that a national standard, imposed in states where local public opinion did not support it, could not succeed. The National Child Labor Committee itself was split on the issue. Edgar Gardner Murphy, who had worked so hard for the cause throughout the South, who indeed had been a leader in founding the National Committee, would not go along with a campaign for a national law and felt so strongly that he resigned from the committee.

But bills had been introduced in Congress annually from 1906 on. In 1916, President Wilson recommended and Congress passed a law prohibiting the shipment in interstate commerce of the products of factories which employed children under fourteen or permitted those from fourteen to sixteen to be employed more than eight hours a day. The Children's Bureau was designated to administer the act—its first assumption of administrative duties.

This first federal child labor law had only a brief existence; it was declared unconstitutional in 1918 in the famous case of *Hammer* v. *Dagenhart*. But in the short period in which it was enforced, policies were laid down and administrative procedures adopted which established a pattern for later national labor legislation—notably the Fair Labor Standards Act of 1938. Grace Abbott, another of the Hull House group, was called by Miss Lathrop to head the new Child Labor Division of the Children's Bureau. Mrs. Kelley hailed the appointment with enthusiasm. Miss Abbott recognized that successful enforcement of the new law hinged on federal-state cooperation. This was in 1916, before similar cooperation was worked out in the field of infant and maternity care. So her development of cooperative methods of administration was entirely pioneering work. As she wrote later, "A basis for cooperation between the Federal and State governments was provided in the Act. The Child Labor Division laid out its plans on the theory that the successful and economical administration of the measure required that this cooperation should be developed into a genuine working relationship." This cooperation was carried out especially in the matter of child labor certificates or "work permits."

Long before 1916, Mrs. Kelley had realized that the

work permit based on documentary proof of age was basic
to an effective child labor law. She had worked to persuade
the states to strengthen their permit systems. Now she had
the satisfaction of seeing Grace Abbott build on these state
permits to enforce the federal law. The new federal act
authorized the Children's Bureau to accept state work permits where the state system was good and well enforced.
The Bureau had long studied the systems used in the various
states and knew which were good and which inadequate.
To begin with, Miss Abbott accepted the permits of thirty-
nine states. In the other states, federal child labor certificates for the fourteen-to-sixteen-year group were issued, but
state agencies were helped and encouraged in every way to
meet the standards so that they could take over the certifying job, and some of them reached that point in the short
period the federal act lasted. Thus the federal law was used
by the Children's Bureau as a lever to improve state administration.

Mrs. Kelley, of course, took the liveliest interest in Grace
Abbott's work. She had been actively trying to raise child
labor standards for twenty years, since her days as Chief
Inspector of Factories for Illinois. Now a fairly adequate
standard had been achieved which covered the whole
United States. It was being administered, she knew, with
integrity and statesmanship. Thus the decision which held
the first federal child labor law unconstitutional was a personal blow to Mrs. Kelley. Once before, in 1895, she had
seen her work struck down by a court decision—when the
Illinois Supreme Court held the state's eight-hour law for
women invalid. Now the highest court in the land, by a
five-to-four vote, destroyed the national minimum for children which had been enacted by Congress after years of
widespread public discussion and demand. Florence Kelley
was hotly indignant at this judicial block to social progress.

A second attempt at national action against child labor—

this time through use of the Congressional power to tax —was likewise held unconstitutional in 1922.

Then Mrs. Kelley and other proponents decided their only course was to secure an amendment to the federal Constitution specifically authorizing Congressional action in this field. Into the campaign for the child labor amendment, Mrs. Kelley threw herself with the utmost vigor. In 1924, Congress finally passed the amendment by the necessary two-thirds in each house. Next came the campaign for ratification in the states. A few states ratified promptly, none of them in the industrial East. Rather surprisingly, opposition was bitter in many states with child labor standards higher than those of the federal laws which had been held unconstitutional. Many of us had expected support for ratification of the amendment in states like Massachusetts, where talk of unfair competition from child-employing industry in the South had been rife. No law which Congress might pass under authority of the amendment would raise child labor standards in a state like Massachusetts. Rather, like the two short-lived federal acts which had been destroyed by the courts, a new law could be expected to drive children out of the textile mills of the South. So Massachusetts, which had been complaining that the textile industry was moving South to escape Massachusetts labor laws, ought logically to have welcomed the child labor amendment. Instead, in Massachusetts and also in New York the fight against ratification was bitter.

Some of the opposition came from a genuine belief that under our federal form of government responsibility in a field such as labor standards should be left to the states. Some of it was due to mounting dissatisfaction with the Prohibition Amendment. The attempt to outlaw liquor through national action was certainly a failure. Should it then be tried for child labor? In the main, however, reactionary forces which wished to perpetuate child labor in the South fought the amendment by whipping up the fear of

communism and radicalism. The amendment was attacked
as "Russian in origin," as "fathered by socialists, commu-
nists, and bolshevists." It would "nationalize the children
of the land and bring about in this country the exact conditions which prevail in Russia." Rather unexpectedly to
many of us, Catholic opposition became intense. It was
alleged that the amendment would "destroy parental control
over children." Even Governor Alfred E. Smith of New
York turned against the amendment when the position of
his church became clear.

In the fight for ratification from 1924 until Mrs. Kelley
died in 1932, many of us reluctantly found ourselves in
rather serious disagreement with her as to strategy. To secure favorable action in the necessary thirty-six states, we
urged avoiding the East where the opposition seemed most
intense and where the Catholic clergy were leading a bitter
fight against ratification. The Middle West and Far West
seemed to us much more hopeful territory. To this proposal
Mrs. Kelley turned a deaf ear. She was determined to follow
the precedent set in the fight for woman suffrage. In 1917
the New York Suffrage party had presented to the New York
Legislature a monster petition of over a million signatures.
It was universally believed that this had forced favorable
action on woman suffrage in the New York Legislature and
had been of immense influence nationally.

Mrs. Kelley was determined to repeat this maneuver and
present the New York Legislature with a similar monster
petition demanding ratification of the child labor amendment. In March, 1925, she wrote Julia Lathrop: "For New
York and New Jersey I think there is not a minute to lose beginning work on a copy of Mrs. Catt's old petition. It took 2
years and was laid before the legislature with 1,030,000 signatures—although the petition observed the forms of a plea,
it was in reality an appalling warning to the legislature, even
though women signers in those days were not yet voters."

To this end Florence Kelley drove herself relentlessly,

and strained almost to the breaking point the slender financial resources of the Consumers League through the engagement of a special "petition secretary" and other added help.

To those of us who disagreed with the wisdom of her course, our difference of opinion was painful. Often enough we had differed on details; we knew Mrs. Kelley's frailties as well as her strength. We were well aware of her tendency to be carried away by the enthusiasm of the moment into extremes of action. But we had always felt confident that the basic truth of her policies and her utterances far outweighed any errors in detail. Now we found ourselves in disagreement over an important issue. Many of the Consumers League board of directors doubted the efficacy of trying to repeat the monster petition strategy which had proved so successful in the woman suffrage fight. In any case, the cost was prohibitive. Mrs. Kelley's courage in the face of financial deficits had always been dauntless. She counted on deficits being made up some way or other by the unremitting work of successive financial secretaries, and she was usually proved right. Emily Sims Marconnier, above all others, was a genius at raising money for the League. But the cost of the monster petition to push ratification of the child labor amendment in New York State went beyond reason. For once Mrs. Kelley's board refused to follow her lead, and to her great resentment put a stop to this ill-advised effort.

At the time of her death in 1932, only six states had ratified the amendment. Though many more ratified in the thirties—when depression conditions and the New Deal combined to revive this campaign—the necessary thirty-six states were never secured. When the Fair Labor Standards Act of 1938, setting child labor as well as wage and hour standards for workers "in interstate commerce," was finally upheld by the U. S. Supreme Court (thus overruling the *Hammer* v. *Dagenhart* decision), the need for the amendment was largely over. At long last a national minimum of protection to children in most occupations was secured. To be sure, children in agriculture, especially the children of migratory workers who pick the crops, are still worked too young and too long hours. But throughout the land factory employment of children under sixteen is prohibited. The work permit based on documentary proof of age, issued by state authorities, is a basic feature of the administrtaion of this federal law. Many "workers in the vineyard," and changing attitudes among employers, contributed over the years to this result; but no one individual played a bigger part than Florence Kelley.

Chapter 11

Industry in the Tenements

Florence Kelley's earliest knowledge of industrial home-work came when she saw the survival of cottage nailmaking and chainmaking in England in 1883. This kind of industrial work was then regarded as a remnant of the "putting-out" or domestic system of manufacture which had preceded the Industrial Revolution. The putting-out system had never been general in the United States, and Florence probably assumed, at the time, that this kind of exploitation did not exist in her own country where manufacturing was done by machinery in factories.

When she went to live in Hull House she found differently. She discovered a wide variety of manufacturing processes carried on in the surrounding tenements under squalid and unsanitary conditions, where workers were paid such low piece rates that they were forced to work long hours and to use the labor of the youngest children. As already narrated, she was instrumental in getting the Illinois Legislature to take action.

As Chief Inspector of Factories for Illinois she tried hard to enforce the regulations she had helped to secure for the control of homework. But in common with labor officials in other states, she concluded that only a total removal of manufacturing from the tenements could solve the problem. And when she became general secretary of the Consumers League, she would gladly have worked to obtain prohibitory legislation. But this solution seemed impossible, for the highest court in New York had in 1885 held unconstitutional a law prohibiting the manufacturing of cigars in tenements.[1]

Cigar making was probably the first American industry in which tenement manufacture became a serious problem. The attempt to end it by law, though antedating Florence Kelley's career, had such an effect on this part of her activities that it deserves a place in her story. Cigar making had been a highly skilled trade, but in 1869 a wooden mold was introduced which greatly lessened the skill required. At the same time, the demand for cheap cigars was increasing. Many cigar makers were emigrating to this country. This combination of factors led to the growth of tenement manufacturing of cigars in New York City during the seventies, with all the evils typical of industrial homework. One official report said that everybody in the cigar-maker's family worked—children of all ages being obliged to spend eight to ten hours a day stripping the tobacco leaves for their parents.

The president of the Cigar Makers' Union was Samuel Gompers (this was before the American Federation of Labor was established, of which he was to become president). Gompers and his union made a determined struggle against this system of cigar making, because they realized that it killed craft skill and demoralized the industry. They stressed the hazard to health in smoking cigars made under the terribly unsanitary conditions in the vermin-infested tenements. And they sought a law to prohibit the evil.

In 1883 Theodore Roosevelt was serving his first term in the New York Legislature. He was appointed to a com-

---

[1] In re Jacobs 98 N.Y. 98 (1885). At that time, under the rules of the U. S. Supreme Court, the state could not appeal this case to Washington.

mittee to investigate the situation, and was shown through the tenements by Gompers. The scenes he witnessed were, he said, revolting. The proposed law ran counter to all the principles of *laissez faire* to which he was committed, but the actual situation persuaded him. "Whatever the theories might be," he wrote, "as a matter of practical common sense I could not conscientiously vote for the continuance of the conditions which I saw. . . . Instead of opposing the bill, I ardently championed it."[2] The bill passed the legislature and Roosevelt represented the Cigar Makers' Union in urging Governor Grover Cleveland to sign it. This New York law of 1883 was the first to prohibit any kind of industrial homework.

At once the employers in the cigar industry determined to test the validity of the new act, and in January, 1885, it was unanimously declared unconstitutional by the highest court of the state of New York. The court held that the act was not related to the public health and that in passing it the legislature had unduly interfered with private property. It was this decision, Theodore Roosevelt wrote in later years, which first awakened him to the fact that judges "knew legalism, but not life."

This decision brought more and more homework into the tenements. When I worked with Mrs. Kelley, the lower East Side of New York was full of it. Children of kindergarten age sat with their elders for hours on end stripping tobacco leaves, pulling out basting threads, twisting artificial flowers and feathers, or shelling nuts. I remember going into rooms piled high with garments or other goods to be finished, where whole families worked with such urgency that even the children seemed reluctant to raise their eyes from their task.

As industrial homework increased and extended from one industry to another, a number of states, debarred from prohibiting it, attempted to control it through regulation.

---

[2] Theodore Roosevelt, *An Autobiography* (New York, 1926), p. 80.

Beginning with Massachusetts in 1891, New York in 1892, and Illinois in 1893, twelve states acted before the decade ended. But could regulation be effective in eliminating even the worst abuses? Mrs. Kelley had tried her best to enforce the Illinois law, but felt the job virtually impossible. When she came to New York she had a two-fold interest. The Consumers League, of course, wanted these laws strengthened and enforced. Besides, its label for white underwear was supposed to guarantee that the goods had not been finished in tenements. Unless these laws were enforced, how could the League give this guarantee? In Massachusetts Mrs. Kelley felt some confidence in the Labor Department's work; in New York, she found that chaos reigned. Homeworkers were supposed to obtain licenses to work on specified articles, and their homes were supposedly subject to sanitary inspection. Manufacturers were supposed to register the addresses of their homeworkers. But what was actually happening? Anybody could see the piles of bundles carried, mountain high, into the tenements. The visiting nurses with whom Mrs. Kelley lived at Miss Wald's settlement reported innumerable families sick with communicable disease who were working on garments and other objects—entirely without the required licenses or sanitary inspection. Mrs. Kelley asked Dr. Annie F. Daniels, a physician of nineteen years' practice in the tenements, to speak to the Consumers League in 1902. In her report, Mrs. Kelley summarized the speech: "During the past year, in 179 tenements in which she [Dr. Daniels] saw garments being made while she visited patients, she saw less than six licenses framed and hung as the law requires." In addition to the uncounted unlicensed homeworkers, the Labor Department reported that there were 20,000 licensed groups of workers. However, the department refused Mrs. Kelley access to these lists, and she had to work for three years to get the department to change its methods and make these lists public records. Meanwhile, tenement work was growing like a mushroom. There were now 62,390 persons licensed to do homework in 30,000 different tenements, but thirty-nine inspectors for the whole state. Naturally, inspection was farcical. Mrs. Kelley thus illustrated what was happening:

In the vain effort to enforce partial restrictions which are in the nature of the case non-enforceable, a provision was enacted in 1899 requiring a license from the factory inspector for every person or group of persons who worked at any process of manufacture of some thirty articles, in any tenement house or in a building in the rear of one.

After this provision had been in force for five years, the writer one day in 1904 observed a woman walking along Mulberry Street, New York, carrying a huge bundle of knee pants on her head. The burden bearer mounted to the fifth floor of an Italian tenement and threw her bundle upon a singularly greasy kitchen table. Asked to show her license to work, she brought out, with the friendly smile and courteous manner of the Sicilian peasant woman, a letter from the New York State Department of Labor, dated some seven weeks before, notifying her that her premises were unfit for licensing, and that no more work must be done in them until they had been thoroughly cleansed, reinspected, and licensed. The cheerful needlewoman, unable to read in any language, but reassured by the seal of the State of New York on the envelope, had assumed that this was the license for which she had been told to apply, and had worked away happily in the consciousness of having obeyed the law.[3]

With homework prohibition unconstitutional, Mrs. Kelley tried to think of a more workable form of regulation. Something might be done at least to insure more sanitary conditions by requiring the landlord, rather than the individual homeworker, to secure a license. The Commissioner of Labor in cooperation with local boards of health, and in New York City with the new Tenement House Department, might license a building and hold the landlord responsible for sanitary conditions. Mrs. Kelley got Lawrence Veiller, who had been deputy commissioner of the New York Tene-

---

[3] *Some Ethical Gains Through Legislation* (New York, 1905), p. 237.

ment House Department, to draft a bill on these lines, and it was enacted in 1904. With this new law, a vigorous new head of the Labor Department, and some additional deputies, Mrs. Kelley was able to report some improvement. "Mr. Sherman's modern and strenuous methods," she wrote, "are both diminishing the extent to which tenement house work is carried on in the most undesirable streets . . . and stimulating improvements in some tenements in these streets until they meet the requirements of the law and receive licenses. In both directions, this is clear gain for the community."

Better enforcement in New York drove tenement work to New Jersey, and we find Mrs. Kelley urging the Consumers League of New Jersey to direct their efforts toward similar legislation there. The executive secretary of the New Jersey League made a study entitled "Factory Work in Newark Homes." In New York, Mrs. Kelley herself made an investigation long overdue into food manufacturing in tenements. Until this time, no foods had been included among the thirty-two specified articles which, according to law, could not be manufactured in unclean and unlicensed tenements. Following Mrs. Kelley's exposure, the legislature extended the list to include "the manufacturing, preparing, and packing of macaroni, spaghetti, ice cream, ices, candy confectionery, nuts and preserves."

A real advance in the matter of industrial homework in New York came as one of the reforms advocated by the famous Factory Investigating Commission set up in that state after the disastrous Triangle Fire in 1911. (This commission was led by two young men who in later years became important political figures and outstanding advocates of labor legislation—Alfred E. Smith, later Governor of New York, and Robert F. Wagner, who became U. S. Senator.) The commission succeeded in largely revamping the labor laws of New York between 1912 and 1915. As for tenement homework, its investigation showed sixty-two articles (beyond the forty-one then subject to licensing) being processed by homeworkers. Because of the hardships that might result, the commission was deterred from recommending that the whole system be rooted out at once, but it did recommend several important amendments to the law.

Most important, the new law completely prohibited tenement manufacturing of certain specified articles. The 1885 decision holding prohibition of cigar manufacturing in tenements unconstitutional had never been overruled. But the court had apparently reached its conclusion because it could see no protection to public health in such a prohibition. Now the New York Legislature declared that protection of the public health required the prohibition of tenement manufacturing of the following articles: "Food products, dolls, doll clothing, and infants' and children's wearing apparel." Medical authorities might differ as to the method of transmission of various diseases, but there seemed at least a reasonable danger to public health in the manufacturing of these articles in living quarters with the likely proximity of contagious and infectious sickness. As Mrs. Kelley wrote by way of illustration: "Although we do not know precisely how poliomyelitis is carried, few persons would willingly use articles made by the patient's bedside. Yet manufacturing was carried on throughout the epidemic in houses in which patients suffered and died from this plague."

The list of prohibited articles was brief. It did not touch the great bulk of tenement manufacturing. But at least a breach had been made in the walls. For the first time in any state, certain articles were to be cleared out of the tenements altogether.

Another amendment to the industrial homework law gave Mrs. Kelley great satisfaction. The minimum age and maximum hours of the Child Labor Law were applied to children working at home. How well this could be enforced was an open question. But the determination to do something to prevent this use of young children was a step forward. Mrs. Kelley rejoiced, but knew well that the fight against the evils of industrial homework was far from won.

A few years later she got a chance to strike another and even more effective blow, this time on a national scale. It was soon after our entry into the First World War. A young man came to Mrs. Kelley's office to ask her help. He was Sidney Hillman, recently elected president of the Amalgamated Clothing Workers of America. He told her that homework, which his union had worked hard to abolish in the men's clothing industry, was again increasing rapidly. In the great clothing centers—New York, Chicago, Rochester—piles of men's clothing were again being carried into the tenements for finishing, and the same thing was happening in many remote districts. This clothing was Army uniforms; the United States government was a party to this breakdown of hard-won standards in the industry.

Mrs. Kelley promptly offered to go to Washington with Mr. Hillman to help him lay the situation before the Secretary of War—who by a happy coincidence was also the president of the National Consumers League. Newton D. Baker had succeeded John Graham Brooks to that office in the League in 1915. Baker had been mayor of Cleveland, and, before that, city solicitor under Tom Johnson—who made Cleveland famous as the best governed city in the United States. As city solicitor, Baker had successfully enforced a new and controversial provision of the Ohio Child Labor Law prohibiting employment of children after 6:00 P.M. Mr. and Mrs. Baker had long been members of the Consumers League of Ohio and great believers in Florence Kelley. When he became Secretary of War he asked Mrs. Kelley whether he should resign as president of the National Consumers League. "She thought not," he afterwards related. "I considered, and I thought not. She wanted me to carry into the operation of that Department, to the extent it was possible, the spirit for which the Consumers League stood." Now the War Department had become a great employer of labor. Its employees, direct and indirect, included the majority of all industrial employees in the country.

With Mrs. Kelley's help, Sidney Hillman got a chance to tell his story to the Secretary of War. He did not need to labor the point. Newton Baker thoroughly understood the evils of tenement manufacturing. He acted at once. On July 20, 1917, he appointed a committee of three to study conditions in the garment industry affecting the making of uniforms and named Mrs. Kelley one of the three. Louis Kirstein, a well-known industrialist, member of the Wm. Filene & Sons firm in Boston, was made chairman, and Captain W. E. Kreusi, of the Quartermaster's Department, was the third member.

Mrs. Kelley's first reference to this new work—at the annual meeting of the National Consumers League that autumn of 1917—was characteristic. She reported having addressed 171 meetings in fourteen states and added, "The number of meetings and conferences would have been larger but for the fact that I was commandeered by Secretary Baker in July to act on the Committee of Inquiry as to labor standards prevailing in the manufacturing of army clothing."

The committee had acted promptly; appointed on July 20, it reported to Secretary Baker on August 11, substantiating Sidney Hillman's charges.

Large orders for uniforms were being obtained by "mushroom" contractors and contract jobbers. Some of the work had been farmed out in outlying districts, tenements, and poorly equipped makeshift factories. Some contracts had passed through two or three hands and were being executed at a price far less than the government's price, by labor hired at a fraction of the usual wage for such operations. Some of the work was being done in tenements by children who said they were fifteen years old but who had no working papers. Under these conditions, the industry had "escaped for the moment from state factory inspection and other measures of control," the committee said.

These conditions were obviously not new to clothing manufacture, but now, for the first time, measures could be taken to correct them. The Secretary of War formally approved the committee's report, and set up a board of control for labor standards in army clothing, with power to carry out recommendations of the committee. The three members of the committee were appointed to constitute the new board.

The recommendations may be summarized as follows: (a) the adoption of a new form of clothing contract, including terms to insure better deliveries of garments manufactured under decent standards; (b) employment of safeguards to see that bidders were qualified to accept contracts, and to avoid the tendency of giving contracts to sweatshops; (c) the employment of inspectors to supervise enforcement of the contract; (d) preference in letting contracts to manufacturers operating under collective bargaining agreements.

Mrs. Kelley had reason to be satisfied with the report of the committee, and its acceptance. Could the new board now enforce the recommendations? To her share in this new work she devoted most of her time for the next six months.

The War Department, through the quartermaster general, cooperated fully in putting the recommendations into effect. The quartermaster submitted to the new board of control the lists of prospective bidders on clothing. Before bidders' names were certified to the quartermaster, inspectors of the board reported whether or not the proposed bidder maintained satisfactory conditions in his plant and observed the state labor laws. The board further maintained continued inspection of plants to which contracts were awarded. Mrs. Kelley was in the thick of this work. As Secretary Baker later wrote: "From all over the United States, wherever uniforms were in the making or ingredients of uniforms, I heard of Florence Kelley. . . . She had been there on the ground, speaking in the name of the government with that extraordinary authority and decision and clarity and knowledge with which she always spoke."

At the next annual meeting of the National Consumers League in November, 1918, Mrs. Kelley reported with satisfaction that the removal of work on Army clothing from the tenements and from almost all firetrap workshops had been accomplished.

After this temporary if spectacular demonstration of sweatshop control by the federal government, little advance was made to curb industrial homework in Mrs. Kelley's lifetime. For the gains made in recent years, we owe much to her efforts. Above all others she brought out the virtual impossibility of government enforcement of minimum standards for hours, wages, child labor, and sanitation when work is carried on in tenement homes.

Chapter 12

A Floor Under Wages

In 1908 Florence Kelley discovered the weapon she was seeking to fight poverty and substandard wages, especially among women who lacked the protection of union organization. This weapon was the legal minimum wage.

To understand the early success of her efforts to secure minimum wage laws in the United States, we must look at some of the other things she was doing and some of the other things that were happening early in the twentieth century. This was a period when reform and social legislation were in the air. The so-called "muckrakers" were arousing the thinking public to some of the rotten spots in our political and economic life. Insurgency had developed in both political parties, led by Robert La Follette and George Norris among Republicans and Woodrow Wilson as Governor of New Jersey among Democrats. Progressive-minded people in the United States looked at the Lloyd George legislation in England and Beatrice Webb's brilliant minority report as a member of the English Poor Law Commission, and began to realize the need for government action in this country. The Pittsburgh Survey, begun in 1907 and financed by the new Russell Sage Foundation, shocked the public with its revelation of the twelve-hour day, the seven-day week, child labor, and low wages that prevailed in the great steel industry. A federal investigation into the condition of woman and child wage earners in the United States, published in nineteen volumes, aroused public horror at the low earnings of women workers. American complacency was seriously shaken.

Mrs. Kelley, one of the advisory group for the Pittsburgh Survey (along with John R. Commons and Robert A. Woods), took part in its investigations and wrote a section of its report. Day in and day out she exhorted everyone who would listen. Especially, she addressed herself to the professional social workers of the country. Above all other groups, she believed, they should recognize the industrial and economic factors underlying the poverty and disease with which it was their business to deal. Some of them of course saw this as well as she did.

In 1909 Jane Addams became president of the National Conference of Social Work (the first woman, amazingly enough, to hold that office) and set up the Occupational Standards Committee, with Paul Kellogg as its chairman. At the 1910 conference Mrs. Kelley was the featured speaker at a meeting held under the auspices of Paul Kellogg's committee. She declared that our official publications were the laughing stock of more scientifically minded Europeans. Not one state in all the Union recorded the births of all the children. Of women in industry, how many lived at home and were partly supported? How many, on the contrary, were the main support of their families? For lack of adequate information along these lines, charitable effort was "mere fumbling. . . . For want of this knowledge we may provide reformatories for girls when we should be building penitentiaries for their employers," she said.

The next year Mrs. Kelley was herself chairman of the Occupational Standards Committee and secured two speakers for the meeting whose addresses created a stir beyond the social-worker audience who heard them. One was by Dr. Alice Hamilton, who told of the first official move in this country to study occupational diseases. And Louis D. Brandeis made a pioneer address urging a comprehensive system of social insurance to cover the hazards of industrial accidents, invalidity, old age, and unemployment.

At the time of the Brandeis speech in 1911, legislative sessions were urging the first crop of workmen's compensation laws in the United States.[1] But no other kind of social insurance had even been discussed in this country, though much of it was already in operation in Europe. Mr. Brandeis was aroused by the recent disclosures of human wastage in industry. He saw that wage earners could not make themselves financially independent because of the hazards of industry, and without that independence, he declared, they could not be free men. Such evils should at least be minimized "by the state's assuming or causing to be assumed by others, in some form, the burden incident to its own shortcoming." It is noteworthy that he stressed at this early date what became a typically American feature of our social security system. He urged that it could serve as a preventive as well as a palliative. If industry and the community were made to pay the cost of inhuman conditions of labor from day to day, "Consider," he said, "how great would be the incentive to humanize these conditions."

Florence Kelley's own speech at this 1911 meeting centered on the special new kind of labor law which was at the time her primary concern—the minimum wage.

Mrs. Kelley had brought back the minimum wage idea from Europe where she had gone in 1908 as a delegate to the first International Meeting of Consumers Leagues held at Geneva. One of the speakers was J. J. Mallon, who reported on the new British legislation to set up minimum wage boards in sweated industries, which was to go into effect in England in 1910. Such a law was already functioning in Australia. In these countries it was not limited to

[1] Except for the New York law of 1910 which was promptly held unconstitutional by the New York courts.

women, but Mrs. Kelley seized upon this new method of dealing with the basic evil of underpay as particularly applicable to those workers with whose plight she was preoccupied—unorganized girls and women. She came home afire with this new idea, pledged in her own mind to its adoption in this country.

She presented the minimum wage idea to the National Consumers League at its annual meeting in 1909, and the delegates voted to recommend that state and local leagues study the subject with a view to a legislative campaign in 1910. A special League committee on the minimum wage was set up, consisting of Professor Arthur Holcombe of Harvard, Professor Emily Greene Balch of Wellesley, and Father (later Monsignor) John Ryan of St. Paul Theological Seminary. Father Ryan had an especially important influence in the spread of minimum wage legislation. In 1910 the National Consumers League made the minimum wage a part of its ten-year program.

In her speech to the social workers in 1911, Mrs. Kelley declared that a legal minimum wage was a necessary accompaniment to a shorter hours' law. She recounted how the garment manufacturers and cotton mill men had appeared before the New York Legislature a few months earlier "to oppose the women's 54 hour bill upon the plea that the workers could not live upon their earnings if their hours were shortened—the same plea," she added, "that is urged against shorter hours for little children in Georgia where they work 66 hours." For unorganized women and child workers she asserted, "Society itself must build the floor beneath their feet, and no other effective floor has hitherto been invented for their safety than the minimum wage boards in force for eighteen years in Australia and for eighteen months in England." She recognized the constitutional difficulties confronting her new proposal and boldly threw her challenge at the courts: "If it be true that these boards cannot be created because we have an eighteenth-century constitution interpreted by nineteenth-century judges, then the urgent need of this Republic is for a twentieth-century constitution interpreted by twentieth-century judges. But is the trouble really in the constitution, or is it in the judges?"

While she spoke, some progress was already being made. Largely due to Consumers League impetus, minimum wage bills and resolutions to investigate women's wages were introduced in legislative sessions in a number of states in 1911. In Wisconsin the bill was introduced in the Senate by a young man who had just come from graduate study with Father Ryan, and in the Assembly by another young man whose mother was president of the Wisconsin Consumers League. This bill, however, was not passed. In Kentucky, at the instance of the Consumers League of that state, the governor appointed a commission to investigate the working conditions of women. The Connecticut Legislature authorized a similar investigation. In Massachusetts the state branches of the Consumers League, the Women's Trade Union League, and the American Association for Labor Legislation organized a committee in late 1910 to work for an official investigation of women's wages.

Mrs. Glendower Evans, close friend of Mrs. Kelley, played a decisive part in the Massachusetts story. In a sketch she wrote later, she told how Mrs. Kelley had involved her in the minimum wage fight.

"I remember a meeting at the Women's Trade Union League in October, 1910," wrote Mrs. Evans, "which [we] attended together after she had lunched at my house. There was also present at luncheon J. R. Clynes, M.P., later a member of the British labor cabinet, who went with us to the meeting. Mr. Clynes told what the minimum wage law had accomplished in Great Britain by putting a bottom to wages below which they could not be forced down."

The Massachusetts Legislature in 1911 passed a bill to set up a Commission of Inquiry, and Mrs. Evans was dismayed to find herself appointed by the governor as one of the five members. She felt totally unequipped. "At that time I was so preoccupied with the Massachusetts reform schools to which I was giving my very life that I drew no deductions from Mrs. Kelley's talk." She felt dimly that she should keep out of industrial struggles because she knew that her sympathies would range her with the workers "apart from the merits of the case." However, she had been appointed to the commission and she was determined to see it through. The appropriation provided was totally inadequate for any investigation, so she began by raising additional funds to enable the commission to make real inquiry. Even more important, she secured the appointment of Mary W. Dewson as executive secretary. This was Mary Dewson's first appearance in industrial investigation, in which she was to become well known. Mrs. Evans had gauged her caliber in parole work in the girls' reform schools of Massachusetts. She established Mary Dewson and her small staff on a floor of her beautiful house, looking out over the Charles River.

By the end of the winter, Miss Dewson had completed a thorough study of wages in four industries: candy factories, laundries, department stores, and textiles. In all these industries the earnings of the girls and women studied were convincingly shown to be far below minimum costs of living. Could any legal means along the lines of the British and Australian precedents be devised to check this exploitation?

"Many a time did my heart faint while this wage inquiry was in process, for I was slow to see how a minimum wage could be made to work," wrote Mrs. Evans. "But what will Florence Kelley say and all the social workers from Jane Addams down, if I say that minimum wage legislation is not practical? Social workers all over the country are looking to me to back up Mrs. Kelley; how if I should turn it down?"

It was Arthur Holcombe, chairman of Mrs. Kelley's new Minimum Wage Committee, who persuaded Mrs. Evans of the practicability of a minimum wage law. Four of the five members of the Massachusetts commission agreed upon a bill modeled on the English act providing for wage boards to be established for separate industries. A new element in the proposed law was the inclusion of representatives of the public as well as representatives of employers and employees on each board. This recognition of the consuming public in fixing wages has remained a characteristic of all subsequent minimum wage legislation in the United States.

If Mrs. Evans, in spite of all her sympathies, had for a time questioned the feasibility of this new measure, the members of the Massachusetts Legislature were far more dubious. Mrs. Kelley attended some of the hearings on the bill in a fever of impatience for action, "if we and not our grandchildren are to realize this hope," as she once said.

At that moment of indecision, something happened which tipped the scales, and the Massachusetts legislators were pushed into daring action. It was in the spring of 1912 that the great textile strike at Lawrence was at its height, precipitated by the excessively low wages paid.

"The whole country was aroused by that strike," wrote Mrs. Evans, "while the workers in the cotton and woolen mills, made up of many nationalities, walked the streets in their thousands and assembled in great parades. Violence followed, and the arrest and trial of Ettore and Giovanetti for murder became a national scandal.

The coincidence of this great strike and the publication of the report of the Minimum Wage Commission made history. It focused attention, as nothing else could have, on the minimum wage bill before the legislature and forced its passage much more quickly than any of its original sponsors had thought likely.

The Massachusetts law was passed in June, 1912. While it was a great victory, and brought the minimum wage into the realm of practical politics, this pioneer law contained major concessions to the opponents of such legislation. It instructed wage boards in setting rates for the various industries to consider not only the minimum cost of living but also the "financial condition of the industry," a serious limitation to the setting of adequate rates. And there were no penal provisions in the act. Employers who refused to pay the minimum wage rates established for their industry had nothing to fear except the publication of their names in a newspaper. It was hoped that the pressure of public opinion would force compliance. Even with these weakening provisions, the Massachusetts law was a radical innovation. Australia, where this remedy for low wages was in use, was very far away, and cottage chainmaking, the first industry to which it was applied in England, sounded remote and outlandish to most Americans—though it awakened vivid memories for Florence Kelley, carrying her back to the walking trip through the Midland counties with her father in 1883.

Yet, in 1913, eight states followed the Massachusetts example—or rather outdid it, passing minimum wage laws for women and minors without the weakening features of the Massachusetts law.

For a variety of reasons the time was ripe for this amazing achievement. But one of these reasons, and an important one, was the long and patient work which Mrs. Kelley had been carrying on to awaken the country to the condition of women wage earners. Her education of the professional social workers bore amazing fruit in 1912. In their annual meeting in Cleveland that year, the social workers went a step beyond hearing speeches on industrial matters. They adopted a program of industrial minimums covering minimum wages, maximum hours, safety and health, etc., which had been drawn up by Florence Kelley, Jane Addams, Paul Kellogg, and Samuel Lindsay. A few weeks later this program was (to quote Jane Addams) "swept into the insurgent political movement." Two years before, Theodore Roosevelt had come back from big game hunting in Africa and plunged again into politics. In 1912 he "threw his hat into the ring," as he termed it. When he failed to win the Republican nomination for president, the Progressive (Bull Moose) party was launched and he was acclaimed its candidate. He took over the social workers' program of industrial minimums and made it part of his platform. Paul Kellogg told the story.

"This report was all grist to T. R.'s mill in launching the Progressive party during that summer. Through the initiative of John Kingsbury, we had a session with him out at Oyster Bay. I wrote some paragraphs which he more or less put into his keynote speech at the Chicago Convention; and he took over the Cleveland program of standards of life and labor practically bodily, and it was, as you know, incorporated in the Progressive party."

As the *New York Times* put it: "During the campaign Colonel Roosevelt, who had let Miss Jane Addams and her colleagues write his social welfare plank, made his strongest appeal to the public on that issue."

Woodrow Wilson, the Democratic party candidate for President, also took an interest in social welfare legislation. After his election he met with a group of social workers, including Mrs. Kelley, who asked his approval of specific measures to be introduced into the new Congress. In his reply, Wilson welcomed the cooperation of the social worker group, saying that he wanted above all to enjoy their confidence and to have at his service the information and counsel of all who were engaged in fundamental social activities. "Most of the vitality of public action," he said, "comes from outside the government. The government does not originate. It responds to public opinion. You are to regard yourselves as forces playing upon the government, and I hope that during the next four years you will find a sensitive part of the government at the top."

In 1912 a milestone was thus reached, when improvement in the conditions of wage earners found a prominent place in the councils of the two chief political parties. The Bull Moose movement, with its almost evangelical fervor, did much to make minimum wage a national issue and thus helped secure eight state laws in 1913. As Arthur Holcombe analyzed it later: "Mrs. Kelley always used to talk of the movement as a 'ten-year program,' and but for the unexpected early action of the Massachusetts Legislature, followed by the organization of the Progressive party in the summer of 1912, and the nation-wide publicity which that party gave to the minimum wage, it is unlikely that legislation would have been adopted so soon in so many states. We were certainly greatly favored by accidental circumstances."

But Professor Holcombe fully realized the major part which Mrs. Kelley had played. "The movement for the legal minimum wage in this country began with Mrs. Florence Kelley," he wrote. "I think every statement of the early history of the minimum wage movement should give [her] the most credit."

Characteristically, Mrs. Kelley herself gave chief credit to the *facts* of low wages—which, once known, led to the public demand for government action to put an end to them. She said years later that the demand for this [Massachusetts] statute and the eight which followed in other states in 1913 arose out of public horror at the low earnings of women workers, as revealed by current studies by the federal government in 1907-10, followed by similar studies by individual states and private organizations.

What happened after 1913? For a variety of reasons the movement which had started so auspiciously slowed down and rumbled to a halt. The First World War, rising wages, doubts as to constitutionality, the reaction against labor legislation in the "return to normalcy" of the twenties all contributed. Probably the constitutionality doubt played the largest role. That is a long story told in detail in a later chapter. No substantial further spread of minimum wage legislation occurred until the thirties, when depression and the vicious spiral of descending wages created a new and urgent demand for action. At last in 1937 the U. S. Supreme Court finally accepted minimum wage laws as a proper exercise of state police power, and Congress dared to pass the federal Fair Labor Standards Act of 1938 which established a nation-wide "floor" for wages.

Chapter 13

The Brandeis Brief

On November 14, 1907, Florence Kelley and I were ac-
tors in a little scene which, though of course we did not
realize it then, marked a turning point in American social
and legal history. We had come to Boston to see my brother-
in-law, Louis D. Brandeis, then a practicing attorney in Boston, and we sat in the back library of his home on a little
street called Otis Place, overlooking the widening of the
Charles River in Back Bay. We had come to ask Mr. Brandeis to appear in the Supreme Court of the United States
to defend the Oregon ten-hour law for women, attacked as
unconstitutional under the Fourteenth Amendment. The
case—soon to become famous—was *Muller* v. *Oregon.*

Mr. Brandeis looked out over the river. "Yes," he said,
thoughtfully, "I will take part in the defense." Thus began
that collaboration between Mr. Brandeis and the Consumers
League which gave a revolutionary new direction to judicial
thinking, indeed to the judicial process itself. Mrs. Kelley,
who had seen her work in Illinois in protecting women from
excessive hours of labor destroyed by an adverse court decision, whose attempt to mitigate the evils of industrial
homework was frustrated by a similar decision in New York,
had now found a champion to fight her battles in the courts
—with, as it proved, magnificent success.

Back of that quiet scene in the Brandeis library lay a
long chain of events in courts throughout the land, and
Mrs. Kelley's increasing recognition that the work to which
she was giving her life was doomed to failure unless something happened to change the attitude of the courts. Her
direct experience with what judges could do to destroy labor
legislation had begun in 1895 when the Supreme Court of
Illinois, in the first Ritchie case, declared invalid the eight-
hour law for women which she was working so hard to enforce. Ignoring a Massachusetts decision of 1876 upholding
a women's hour law, the Illinois court found the statute in
conflict with the state constitution and the Fourteenth
Amendment to the federal Constitution.[1] Thus, said Mrs.
Kelley, "the measure passed to guarantee the Negro from
oppression has become an insuperable obstacle to the protection of women and children." She was especially indignant
at one sentence in the opinion. "There is no reasonable
ground," said the court, "at least none which has been made
manifest to us in the argument of counsel, for fixing eight
hours in one day as the limit."

Mrs. Kelley declared that this view as to the constitutionality of hour laws must and could be changed: "When the
observation of a few years has convinced the medical profession, the philanthropists, and the educators, as experience
has already convinced the employees themselves, that it is
a life and death matter for the young people who form so
large a proportion of their number to have a working day
of reasonable length guaranteed by law, it will be found
possible to rescue the Fourteenth Amendment . . . from the
perverted application upon which this decision rests."[2]

A few years later the prospects seemed brighter. Utah,
having included in its state constitution an article specifically authorizing passage of labor laws by the legislature,

---

[1] *Ritchie* v. *People*, 155 Ill. 98 (1895).

[2] Florence Kelley, *Third Annual Report of the Factory Inspectors
of Illinois* for the year ending December 15, 1895, p. 7.

passed in 1896 an eight-hour law for its principal industry, mining. The constitutionality of the act was at once challenged. It was held valid by the Utah Supreme Court and the case was carried to Washington. Upon the final decision in this case hung the future of legislation regulating hours of labor. In the famous case of *Holden v. Hardy*, the highest court of the land broke away from legalistic reasoning and held constitutional, under the police power of the state, the Utah eight-hour law for miners.[3]

In her analysis of the decision, Mrs. Kelley could scarcely restrain her elation. In contrast to the sinister shadow cast by the Ritchie case, she saw a new day dawning. The court had, she wrote, "come to the rescue of the state legislatures." Now they, and not the judiciary had the power to decide which occupations were "sufficiently injurious" to justify restriction of daily hours of work even for adult men.

The great service rendered by the decision in *Holden v. Hardy*

was its destruction of the bogy-man with which state supreme courts had for years been terrifying themselves, and each other, and timorous legislatures, under the name of the Fourteenth Amendment to the Constitution of the United States. Once for all, it is convincingly laid down by this decision that statutes restricting the hours of labor of employees in occupations injurious to the health will not be held unconstitutional by the Supreme Court of the United States on the ground that they are in conflict with the Fourteenth Amendment to the Constitution of the United States.[4]

Years might be consumed, Mrs. Kelley realized, in the work of education and legislation before the full fruits of this judicial decree could be reaped and enjoyed by working people throughout the Republic. The decision in *Holden v. Hardy* only opened the way. It sustained a statute affecting

---

[3] *Holden* v. *Hardy*, 169 U. S. 366.
[4] *Some Ethical Gains Through Legislation* (New York, 1905), p. 152.

only a few hundred men in a state not highly industrialized. But its importance lay, as she recorded with satisfaction, in affording a precedent national in its scope, "whereby may be done over again successfully work which [such as her own in Illinois] had once been done in vain." The 30,000 women in Illinois factories and sweatshops who had been deprived of all protection might yet be rescued from unlimited hours of work.

Mrs. Kelley's final deductions from *Holden* v. *Hardy* are, in the light of future events, worth recording. "Women in the cotton mills," she wrote,

have only to show that the ever-increasing number of spindles and shuttles and the ever-increasing rate of speed required of them by the improvement of machinery, are wearing out their working energy, in order to be entitled to legislative restrictions upon their working hours under the reasoning of this admirable decision. To women driving foot-power machines under the sweating system, and to the employees in countless other occupations, the same reasoning applies.[5]

She ended by urging studies of industry and its physiological effects by the labor bureaus.

But when another hour law came before the U. S. Supreme Court in 1905, in *Lochner* v. *New York*, a maximum ten-hour day for bakers was held unconstitutional. The court apparently had somewhat reconsidered the position it took in *Holden* v. *Hardy*, or at any rate had narrowed the scope of that decision. Mrs. Kelley was quick to point out that the principle established in the Utah case still stood. What the Lochner case emphasized anew was that men's hours of labor could be restricted by statute "only in occupations proven injurious to the health," and in the opinion of the majority of the court (it was a five-to-four decision), the bakers' trade was held not dangerous *enough* to warrant the state's interference. Thus under its police powers a state

---

[5] *Some Ethical Gains Through Labor Legislation* (New York, 1905).

might still, if injury to health could be shown, act to protect its workers from harmful conditions of labor.

Two years later another New York case threw further doubts on the constitutionality of hour legislation. This time the statute involved a night work law for women. Mrs. Kelley strongly favored night work legislation. She believed that night work for young women was injurious to health and dangerous to morals. Moreover, she knew from her experience in Illinois the great difficulty of enforcing a maximum hour law without a legal closing hour.

She was at this time deeply interested in the attempt being made by the International Association of Labor Legislation to outlaw the night work of women in factories by means of an international treaty. After prolonged investigation of the physical, economic, and moral aspects of night work, a conference of fourteen European nations had been held in 1905 and had drawn up a treaty which was ratified, in the course of the next few years, by all but one of the participating countries.

Conditions in the United States presented a marked contrast. Only four states—Massachusetts, New York, Indiana, and Nebraska—had any legislation on night work of women in factories; and in no state was the legislation secure, for in no state had it been tested in the courts.

In 1907 a New York employer named Williams was arrested for violation of the law prohibiting employment of women after 10:00 P.M. The first New York court in which the case was heard promptly declared the law unconstitutional, citing the Illinois decision of 1895 as authority. "Freedom of contract" under the Fourteenth Amendment had won again. The case was appealed and the appellate division again held the law invalid.

Mrs. Kelley felt desperate, frustrated. Had the Utah miners' case after all pointed to no new day? Did judges know nothing of the injury to health suffered by girls and women working overtime until late at night or on all-night shifts, with no possibility of undisturbed sleep by day? She was indignant at the failure of the state attorney general to bring out the significance of the case. She called the brief, written by a third assistant attorney general "a disgraceful exhibition of ignorance."

It cited the New Jersey fifty-five-hour law for women, though that act had been repealed three years before; it failed even to mention the one important favorable court decision recently rendered by the Oregon State Supreme Court. Worst of all, when the case was carried to the next-to-last court in New York, the attorney general made no oral defense. I well remember the day Mrs. Kelley and I went to the courtroom of the Appellate Division in its white marble building on Twenty-fifth Street in New York, for we wished to show by our presence the public's concern in this pivotal case. What was our consternation to find *no* representative of the attorney general present. We had taken for granted that he himself would make this important argument.

Mrs. Kelley pointed out (what was especially true at the time) that women wage earners are "young women. To sacrifice them is to sacrifice the future as truly as the destruction of the working children destroys the future of the nation." Men with the power of the vote could secure shorter hours for themselves for work in hazardous employments. "The miners of Colorado, Utah, Montana, and Arizona have the eight-hour day. It has recently been secured in Missouri." She continued with mounting indignation: "In the absence of all-powerful trades unions of women (and all-powerful trades unions of women are not to be thought of at the present day), there will be no effective restriction upon the hours of labor of women, boys and girls over sixteen years of age until this infamous decision is reversed. . . . It is to be hoped," she ended more sedately, "that this case

will be carried as soon as possible to the Court of Appeals"
(the highest New York court).[6]

The case was carried to the Court of Appeals, but the
verdict of the lower courts was sustained. How we felt about
this decision of the Court of Appeals is shown in a paragraph
I wrote a few years later.

The New York Court of Appeals deliberately ignored all the
broader implications of the case. . . . We seek in vain for that
freer air of statesmanship and understanding which breathes
from the decision of *Holden* v. *Hardy.* In the Williams case, the
court deliberately limited itself to considering "solely" whether
work at 10:20 P.M. (as in the case at bar) was injurious enough
to warrant interference with women's freedom of contract. They
were genuinely concerned because, under the existing law, no
woman could be employed within the prohibited hours for any
period of time "no matter how short." But the issue did not center
on this single narrow aspect of the matter. It stands to reason
that work at 10:20 P.M. is not in itself inherently injurious. But
night work, *as it exists in reality,* does not consist of such isolated
theoretical employment.[7]

One sentence in the decision, however, held a ray of
hope and suggested a task for the Consumers League. The
judge who wrote the Court of Appeals' opinion had thrown
down an unmistakable challenge in these words: "I find
nothing in the language of the section which suggests the
purpose of promoting health except as it might be inferred
that for a women to work during the forbidden hours of the
night would be unhealthful." [8]

I well remember the excitement with which these words
filled us. Never again would we be caught napping. Never
again would we leave the defense of a labor law to an indifferent third assistant attorney general. Somehow we
would see that a better lawyer handled the case, one who
believed in the law and was better prepared to show the

---

[6] From an unpublished memo by Mrs. Kelley.

[7] *Fatigue and Efficiency* (New York, 1912), p. 248.

[8] *People* v. *Williams,* 189 N.Y. 131 (1907).

court why it was needed to protect women's health. Next time would be different!

We had not long to wait. Even while the Williams case was going its discouraging way through the New York courts, a different record was being established in Oregon. A laundry man, Curt Muller, had been arrested in Portland for violation of the state law setting a ten-hour day for women employed in factories and laundries. On appeal, the validity of the act was affirmed by the Supreme Court of Oregon. Muller was carrying his case to the U. S. Supreme Court.

In October, 1907, the Consumers League of Oregon notified us in New York of this prospect. Here was a demonstration of Mrs. Kelley's generalship. Not for nothing had she traveled the length and breadth of the land year after year, preaching Consumers League doctrine "to everyone who will listen." Her voice, with that fiery invective that marked her speeches, had been a constant warning as to the responsibility of consumers, the abuses of child labor and excessive hours of labor, the nullification of labor law.

The Consumers League of Oregon had been formed in 1903. In July, 1906, Mrs. Kelley had spent ten days in Portland speaking daily, as she notes in her report, at public meetings or in private houses. There, as elsewhere, she had met key people. She had formed lasting friendships with members of the Consumers League board. There, as elsewhere, she had enlisted the interest of the leading clergy, preaching during that visit at the Calvary Presbyterian Church and at the big synagogue of which Dr. Stephen Wise was then rabbi. She had become well acquainted with an active young priest, Father Edwin V. O'Hara, later chairman of the Industrial Welfare Commission of the state, and second only to Father John A. Ryan in his militant social views and his friendship for Florence Kelley and the Consumers League.

When the news came that the Muller case was to be

heard by the Supreme Court in Oregon, Mrs. Kelley was away from New York on a speaking trip. On her return she found that the importance of the occasion, the opportunity at our door, had been recognized by the Consumers League board and that, by what seemed to the men of the board a master stroke, an appointment had been made for Mrs. Kelley to call the next day on the foremost lawyer of the city, Joseph H. Choate, to seek to enlist his aid. Much was made of Mr. Choate's eminence as recognized leader of the New York bar. What a feather in the cap of the League and of Mrs. Kelley if by her eloquence she could persuade him to represent us and defend the case!

But Mrs. Kelley saw the matter in a very different light. She was, in fact, indignant at the action taken in her absence. She knew well enough of Mr. Choate's reputation and his notable services to civic causes in New York. But this was totally different. The issues did not involve civic or political corruption, or any problem of high finance or corporation organization to which Mr. Choate had devoted his talents. Here was at stake the welfare of girls and women whom decade by decade Mrs. Kelley saw employed in increasing numbers throughout the country in laundries, in stores, in factories of all descriptions, at processes becoming continually more complex and more dangerous. Year after year an increasing number of young girls in their early bloom and older women were leaving their homes to go out and work because they must.

And back of the human statistics, the labor law itself was also at stake. In her eyes an adequate labor law was essential to any civilized society, providing as it did a way of peace through the democratic process in place of the violence of industrial autocracy. Labor legislation was at once the central core of her life's work and, as she could not too often repeat, the central means for bringing about a more equitable industrial life. What knowledge, what sympathy had

Mr. Choate with all these things? Mrs. Kelley had other plans.

The next morning, I remember, a friend who had worked closely with Mrs. Kelley in drawing up the tenement manufacture law of 1904 came into her office to see her. This was Lawrence Veiller of the Charity Organization Society.

"I hear you are looking for a lawyer for this Oregon case," he began. "Of course, if you can get Mr. Choate, that would hit the bull's eye. You would be getting the leader of the New York bar. But if he refuses, there are others. George Wickersham's a good lawyer. . . ."

Mrs. Kelley was scarlet with anger. Her hands were shaking. "There is just one man whom I wanted for the defense of the next labor case," she said abruptly. "Such a chance may not come soon again. The man I wanted is Louis Brandeis of Boston."

"Hmm," began Mr. Veiller. Then he looked up and recognized the storm signals. "Well, you probably know whom you want," he ended somewhat lamely and withdrew.

Mrs. Kelley well knew Mr. Brandeis' views on the great issues in American life; she knew of his activities in his own community. Indeed, by this time, in the fall of 1907, Mr. Brandeis' public work was already well known throughout the country. But it was not only because of his major part in the fight to preserve public franchises in Boston or for his outspoken enmity against concentration of wealth in the hands of the few throughout the country that Mrs. Kelley wanted Louis Brandeis for this crucial case before the United States Supreme Court. She knew him as a friend of her former assistant in the Illinois factory inspection department, Mary Kenney, now married to Jack O'Sullivan, labor reporter on the *Boston Globe*. Mary Kenney had come to Boston from Chicago as a labor organizer. She had been at the Carnegie Steel Company at Homestead in 1892 and seen the preparations for the terrible strike when workers were shot down and killed by machine guns. She had been through the Haverhill shoe strike of 1894; she was active in all the textile strikes at Lawrence and Fall River. The workers' side in those struggles lost nothing in her telling, and in Mr. Brandeis she had found a deeply attentive listener.

Mr. Brandeis was well acquainted, too, with other close friend of Mrs. Kelley, the Henry Demarest Lloyds, who had come to live in Boston. He had greatly admired Mr. Lloyd's *Wealth Against Commonwealth,* and it was through Mr. Lloyd that Mr. Brandeis had been asked to be one of the lawyers to present the miners' case before Theodore Roosevelt's Anthracite Coal Strike Commission of 1902. There, and in strikes settled by him as counsel to clients in the Massachusetts shoe industry and other trades, Louis Brandeis had had driven home to him what seemed then and ever after the paramount challenge for management, the paramount issue in the lives of working people: regularity of employment. Mrs. Kelley, too, had long seen in seasonal unemployment one of the worst features of unregulated industry. The Brandeises were very intimate friends and virtually next-door neighbors of Mrs. Glendower Evans, with whom Mrs. Kelley's daughter Margaret had lived for two years and where Mrs. Kelley often visited.

Mrs. Kelley and Mr. Brandeis did not always agree. But she felt that he understood the realities of the workers' world. He understood too what was at stake in this first opportunity to test the constitutionality of a women's hour law in the U. S. Supreme Court. My sister and I had been in the habit of consulting him on perplexing points in Consumers League work. He had shared, as Mrs. Kelley knew, our collective indignation over the failure of the New York attorney general to make an oral argument in the Williams case.

But there was still an appointment to be kept with Mr. Choate. How would Mrs. Kelley conduct herself? It was, I confess, with some trepidation on my part that we went Downtown. We went in glum silence, and after a short delay were ushered into Mr. Choate's private office. Mr. Choate received us very courteously and began with some complimentary references to Mrs. Kelley's father. But he was puzzled as to what he had to do with the Oregon law for women; and, he explained, he was also much pressed for time. Mrs. Kelley answered in monosyllables, confusedly. She hardly looked up. Mr. Choate, with some difficulty, finally got the substance of the Muller case.

"A law *prohibiting* more than ten hours a day in laundry work," he boomed. "Big, strong, laundry women. Why shouldn't they work longer?"

Mrs. Kelley quickly seized her opportunity. She looked up with a beaming smile.

"Why not, indeed?" she asked in her most charming manner. "There is much to be said for that view. But I realize that we should not have intruded on your valuable time, Mr. Choate, in this small matter. Pray forgive me. Many thanks and good day."

And with that she rose and swept out of the office, to the relief, I fancy, as well as to the amazement of the great man left standing in the doorway. She was still smiling broadly when we reached the street.

"That's over, thank God," she exclaimed gleefully. "Tomorrow we'll go to Boston."

On the day following our interview, we went to Boston to see Louis Brandeis. What he would say, we had no idea. After all, he had had no hand in shaping the legal record nor in presenting the defense in the state courts. The verdict of the highest court in Oregon was in our favor; but in the U. S. Supreme Court the adverse Lochner decision invalidating an hour law stood menacingly in our path. The time to prepare a brief was very short, probably not more than a month.

Mr. Brandeis listened to Mrs. Kelley's story and agreed to act as unpaid counsel for the National Consumers League in defense of the Oregon ten-hour law for women. He made only one stipulation: he would present a brief and take part in the oral argument only if invited to represent the state of Oregon by the state's attorney in charge of the defense. This stipulation Mrs. Kelley undertook to meet through Consumers League friends in Oregon.

He then outlined what he would need for a brief: namely, *facts*, published by anyone with expert knowledge of industry in its relation to women's hours of labor, such as factory inspectors, physicians, trades unions, economists, social workers. If I could return to Boston within a fortnight with such printed matter, sufficiently authoritative to pass muster, we would then work up the material in the form of a brief.

Mrs. Kelley and I returned to New York with our work cut out for us. A fortnight to amass the necessary documentation—without personnel, money, or anything but a general idea of the foreign literature on the subject and a complete skepticism as to the existence of any comparable material in American publications.

In these days of abundant tools of research, the paucity of our means seems almost laughable. Moreover, we had no time to train assistants. My sister, Pauline Goldmark, then secretary of the New York City Consumers League, Helen Marot of the New York Child Labor Committee, Mrs. Kelley, and a few others gave up every other engagement they could, and I devoted all my time to the search. We spent a hectic fortnight as readers, translators, copyists, turning over a mounting pile of handwritten pages to a few hard-working typists.

In 1907, industrial medicine had not yet been born in the United States. Three years later, when Dr. Alice Hamilton went to the Fourth International Congress on Occupational Poisons, she found the Brussels Congress "for an American . . . not an occasion for national pride." Dr. Gilbert of the Belgian Labor Department, she reported, briefly dismissed the subject of American participation. "It is well known that there is no industrial hygiene in the United States."

Even in the whole foreign literature on industrial hygiene, little attention had then been paid to industrial fatigue, an area which was later to be examined with great care both in Europe and in the United States. My own studies of the subject grew out of this first Oregon brief, for which we were now intent on finding material.

The two libraries to which we turned—Columbia University and the New York Public Library—gave us every facility. Professor E. R. A. Seligman, then chairman of the Library Committee at Columbia, authorized us to take out any reference works needed. "Only not the British Sessional Papers," I can still hear the librarian murmur disconsolately. We should have hesitated to remove volumes so irreplaceable. But remote as the early British papers may seem, it was there in the successive reports of British factory inspectors and British medical commissions, beginning with the First Children's Commission of 1833, that we found what we were seeking—records of experience with long and short hours of labor. French, German, Italian, and Belgian reports also yielded us fruits in this first rapid survey. A few American reports too, especially those from Massachusetts, gave at least intimations of similar experience here.

The usefulness of our compilation, as it grew sizable, aroused skepticism and even amusement among our friends and those whom we consulted, economists as well as lawyers. Who would read through such a mélange? It would never be received by any court, least of all by the U. S. Supreme Court.

I returned to Boston in less than three weeks, and the faithful researchers, Mrs. Kelley among them, continued to send on material, while Mr. Brandeis immediately immersed himself in the conglomerate I had brought and expressed himself as well pleased with the total impression. It now needed to be organized.

We quickly agreed that what emerged from the whole were the contrasting pictures of misery and its alleviation. From the whole sordid, miserable record of exploited workers under unregulated hours, there stood out—clear and luminous—the regeneration that followed a more decent limitation of hours. But could this be shown in a legal document? It could, said Mr. Brandeis, because this part of the brief need not be legal at all. The legal argument he would present briefly in only a page or two. But in presenting the facts we could bring out the contrast buried in our compilation. To make his point he quoted from Shakespeare, as he often did, and recommended Hamlet's method of contrast: "Look here upon this picture, and on this." The familiar quotation told me what he was aiming at.

"Hyperion to a Satyr," I quoted in reply.

"Yes," he said, "that's the idea."

We would contrast evil and good: the dangers to health, safety, morals, and the general welfare from excessive hours; the corresponding benefits from shortened hours. Reiteration of the theme from country after country, state after state, far from being detrimental, was precisely what was needed to round out the picture.

A fortnight proved all too short to reduce our heterogeneous collection to its component parts, introducing each section in as short, concise, and colorless a summary as I could write. The foreign and American legislation which I summarized was also part of the "facts of common knowledge" on which Mr. Brandeis was relying. The laws of nineteen states, besides Oregon, hung on this decision.

And so the first "Brandeis Brief" was completed. Today the Brandeis Brief is so widely copied—the presentation of economic, scientific, and social facts is so generally made part of the legal defense of a labor law—that the boldness of the initial experiment is hard to realize. But in 1907 the use of such facts in a legal brief presented to the Supreme Court was hazardous and venturesome. It broke with tradition in

tradition's citadel. It rested, to be sure, on the accepted doctrine of "judicial notice," but it made an entirely novel use
of that doctrine. To present such a brief evidenced a supreme confidence in the power of truth.

I repeated to Mr. Brandeis the doubts we had heard expressed as to the Supreme Court's willingness to receive
these economic and scientific facts at this stage in the legal
proceedings. He waved these doubts aside, but later I realized he had recognized the possibility that his novel brief
might be rejected. In our next brief he put my name on the
title page as his assistant, despite the fact that I was not a
lawyer, and told me he had wanted to do that in the first
Oregon case but had decided not to risk additional uncon-
ventionality in that first venture.

The first brief created quite a stir—both favorable and
unfavorable. Enthusiasts and skeptics had not long to wait.
The Muller case was reached on January 15, 1908. Mr.
Brandeis and the Oregon state's attorney both argued in defense of the state's ten-hour law for women. On February
24 the court handed down a unanimous opinion holding the
law constitutional.

Almost as exciting to us as the verdict itself was the
court's explicit recognition of the new Brandeis defense.
Said Justice Brewer in his opinion: "It may not be amiss, in
the present case, before examining the constitutional question, to notice the course of legislation as well as expressions
of opinion from other than judicial sources. In the brief filed
by Mr. Louis D. Brandeis, for the defendant in error, is a
very copious collection of all these matters, an epitome of
which is found in the margin." [9]

In the margin were summarized the American and foreign legislation given in the brief and the substance of ex-
tracts from over ninety reports of committees, bureaus of
statistics, commissioners of hygiene, inspectors of factories,
both in this country and in Europe.

---

[9] *Muller* v. *Oregon*, 208 U. S. 412 (1908).

So the first battle was won. Or rather, it may more accurately be said, the first round of the battle. For from this initial decision in 1908 until the state of Washington minimum wage law was finally sustained thirty years later, the tide of opinion in the courts ebbed and flowed. However, in 1908 Mrs. Kelley called the decision in *Muller* v. *Oregon* "epoch-making." It settled the question for Oregon and confirmed the validity of the nineteen other state laws which regulated more or less effectively the working day of women in industry. What filled Mrs. Kelley's cup of joy was the prompt re-enactment of an hour law for women in Illinois, "where," she wrote, "since May, 1895, these workers had been deprived of all protection whatsoever in consequence of the decision of the Supreme Court of Illinois."

The Brandeis Brief in the Muller case, reprinted together with Justice Brewer's opinion, was in great demand from law schools and universities as well as from labor unions and libraries. Far and wide this little volume spread its message of humanity and hope. Gone was the deadening weight of legal precedent. A movement to extend and strengthen women's hour legislation spread over the country.

Chapter **14**

More Conflict in the Courts

Examined today with a cold, appraising eye, the first Brandeis Brief in *Muller* v. *Oregon,* which made such a stir, seems somewhat meager and platitudinous. Were these the great truths, these dangers to health and welfare, for lack of which the courts had confined themselves to fine-spun legal fictions? Well, when first stated, these *were* great truths, however self-evident they may seem today.

Besides, we ourselves were under no illusions as to the material supplied: in the short time at our disposal we had only scratched the surface. While the brief provided once for all a new method of defense and established its basis, it needed immediate reinforcement. For at any time, Mr. Brandeis warned us, new cases might arise needing new defense.

Mrs. Kelley and I immediately applied to the Russell Sage Foundation for an adequate grant, which, thanks to Mr. John M. Glenn's friendly interest, was promptly provided. Mrs. Kelley was all afire for this new venture and encouraged me to devote all my time to it.

During the winter of 1908-09 we had the resources, then, to conduct a more adequate search of the medical and social literature on the world's experience with working hours and the relation of fatigue to work, to health, and to disease.

Our plan was to accumulate data and to collate and print them "as a compendium for use in future legislation and court cases," as I noted in a report written early in 1909.

But the march of events was too quick for us, and that leisurely program was soon wrecked. After the Oregon decision, Illinois, among other states, had enacted a new ten-hour law for women in factories. In September, 1909, an injunction was issued against enforcement of this new act. Ritchie, who had brought the test case in the nineties, again raised the constitutional issue. Here was the first case since Muller's to be defended in a state supreme court, and, in the very court whose decision of thirteen years before stood like a roaring lion in the pathway.

Here was a situation after Mrs. Kelley's own heart: the opportunity at last of seeing the issue joined on her old battleground in Illinois. An invitation to Mr. Brandeis to participate with the state in oral argument and by brief was quickly obtained. To strengthen the defense still further, it was thought desirable that an Illinois lawyer of distinction should also appear on our side. Through the activity of the Illinois section of the American Association for Labor Legislation (of which Professor Ernst Freund was then president), Mr. W. C. Calhoun, newly appointed ambassador to China, consented to join in the oral defense.

Mr. Brandeis' brief again contained only a few pages of legal argument. But now we could make a better showing of the non-legal evidence which we had accumulated during the past year or more. We had the experience of British factory inspectors, year by year, reinforced by that of various Continental countries and of the British Dominions. On pertinent subjects, such as the greater morbidity of working women, the effects of continuance at work during illness, the general nature of fatigue, the predisposition to disease among fatigued workers, the statistics of sickness insurance societies which existed in some foreign countries—on all these allied subjects we had an abundance of new evidence. The whole made up a volume of some six hundred pages.

To present the oral argument Mr. Brandeis made an arduous journey in bitter mid-winter from Washington, D.C., to Springfield, Illinois. He considered this effort to secure a reversal of the old Ritchie decision so essential that he obtained a three-day adjournment of the U. S. Senate's Ballinger investigation, in which he was then immersed, to make the journey.

For Mrs. Kelley no effort seemed too great for this purpose. In April, 1910, a favorable decision upholding the law was handed down.[1] One sentence of the opinion gave Mrs. Kelley special satisfaction. "What we know as men," said the court, "we cannot profess to be ignorant of as judges." The gist of her earlier criticism had been the remoteness of the judges, their failure to allow for the great change whereby Illinois, purely agricultural before, had grown to be the third greatest manufacturing state of the Union. Now, following the precedent of the Muller case—and the facts—they squarely faced the change and spoke a different language.

Mrs. Kelley envisaged the future opened up by this heartening change:

If the National Consumers League had done no other useful thing besides its contribution towards this decision, our eleven years' existence would be justified by this alone. For the thousands of women and girls in Illinois whose fatigue will at once be reduced are by no means the only beneficiaries of this work. All their innumerable successors will profit by it. But this is not all. The old decision has been for fifteen years a baneful influence in every industrial state in the Republic, always raising the question whether, after all, it was wise to spend energy in trying to get legislation of this character when the courts were likely to hold it contrary to the state if not to the federal constitution. This mildewing influence is now at an end, and we can go forward with new hope and assurance.[2]

---

[1] *Ritchie* v. *Wayman*, 244 Ill. 509 (1910).
[2] Florence Kelley, Annual Report for 1910, unpublished.

With the successful conclusion of these two cases, the pattern was laid down for the future defense of labor laws. In the following years we consolidated our gains. Mrs. Kelley, while carrying on all her other activities for the League and other causes, never ceased to follow every step in these cases, and to throw her influence in the scale wherever it was needed.

To meet the expense of printing a large edition of the Illinois brief, she took the lead in raising a special fund. This brief then was available as ammunition wherever danger threatened the now rapidly increasing legislation regulating women's hours of labor. Our procedure was to follow every case made known to us by our constituent leagues or reported in the press.

When we wanted Mr. Brandeis to enter a case—either by submitting a brief or taking part in the oral argument as he did in about a dozen cases—we had to secure an invitation for him to act on behalf of the state involved. He was unwilling to appear without such an invitation, merely as *amicus curiae*. The status of appearing as an official participant on behalf of the state seemed to him an important element of strength for the defense. After the Brandeis Brief had proved successful, Mrs. Kelley and I were sometimes hard put to secure the necessary official invitation; state officials were reluctant to lose any of the credit which they thought might accrue to themselves if they applied the same method alone—however inadequately equipped they were to do so. We had to walk warily indeed to avoid offending such officials. Various amusing encounters in district attorneys' offices remain in my memory, enlivened by picturesque language and shrouded by a haze of rankest cigar smoke. Sometimes recourse to the governor was necessary. Somehow—with one exception—we always managed to secure the official invitation.

In 1910, cases arose in Virginia, Michigan, and Louisiana. Copies of the Illinois brief were supplied for the defense to the appropriate authorities. In all three states the law, following the recent Oregon and Illinois decisions, was upheld as valid.[3]

In 1912, important cases were brought to our attention in Illinois, Ohio, California, and Washington. Three of these cases required new briefs to defend laws covering other occupations besides factories and laundries. In Illinois the ten-hour law had been amended to include mercantile establishments as well as factories. Mr. Brandeis submitted to the Illinois Supreme Court a short brief which I had prepared especially to show conditions of employment in stores. In Ohio, the fifty-four-hour law for women was challenged by the Ohio Manufacturers Association. Again, at the request of the Ohio attorney general, a brief was submitted to the Supreme Court of that state covering a wider range of occupations. Later an appeal was taken to the U. S. Supreme Court, and Mr. Brandeis again appeared before that body in oral defense of the Ohio act. It was sustained in 1914.

A somewhat different category of workers was included in the California eight-hour law for women—that is, student nurses in hospitals. In a factual brief I compiled the facts justifying this inclusion, and in 1915 Mr. Brandeis joined the California attorney general in successfully defending this act before the U. S. Supreme Court.

Meanwhile, something exciting had been happening in the matter of night work laws—the kind of protection for working women which had been destroyed in New York by the Williams decision in 1907.

In the years from 1912 to 1915 New York completely revamped its protective labor legislation as an outgrowth of the Factory Investigating Commission set up after the disastrous Triangle fire in 1911 when nearly 150 girls lost their lives. Frances Perkins (later U. S. Secretary of Labor) was instrumental in obtaining the creation of the commission.

---

[3] In Virginia it was sustained by the lower courts and the case dismissed by the state Supreme Court on a writ of error.

She had been secretary of a committee of safety organized to focus public attention on fire hazards in industry. Under the leadership of Robert F. Wagner (then lieutenant-governor), and Alfred E. Smith (then a state assemblyman), the commission went far beyond fire hazards in its investigations. Among other matters it made a special investigation of night work and the extreme overtime hours of women night workers,[4] and on the basis of its recommendations a new night work law was enacted by the New York Legislature in 1913 prohibiting the employment of women in factories between 10:00 P.M. and 6:00 A.M. The night work clause was carefully drawn so as to meet, if possible, the objections of the New York Court of Appeals in the Williams case of 1907. By this time, of course, the U. S. Supreme Court had upheld several maximum hour laws for women, beginning with its unanimous decision in *Muller* v. *Oregon.* But the prohibition of night work was obviously a different matter; no case on that subject had reached the Supreme Court. I well remember heated arguments over the wisdom of passing a law which went counter to the opinion of the highest court of the state. Eminent lawyers were certain that the new night work law would promptly meet the same fate as the old one. It took courage for the Factory Investigating Commission and its legal counsel to disregard these views. As expected, the new statute was soon challenged in the Schweinler Press case which was argued in the New York Court of Appeals in 1914.

Adopting the technique of the Brandeis Brief, the New

---

[4] For instance, agents of the commission visited a large twine works employing about 150 women, ten hours at night from 7:00 P.M. to 5:00 A.M. They also visited these women in their homes and reported on their physical and domestic conditions. Most of them were married, averaged about four and one-half hours of sleep by day, and were in poor physical shape.

In corroboration of its own findings, the commission included in its report similar evidence in contemporary investigations, federal and private, on the extreme overtime at night of women in laundries, bookbinding, paper box factories, and other occupations in New York State.

York attorney general incorporated in his brief a large part of the investigating commission's report on night work. In addition, Mr. Brandeis presented to the court a summary of the "facts of knowledge" from some four hundred pages which I had assembled, giving all state and foreign legislation on night work for women, and the world's experience in dealing with its physical, moral, and economic effects.

On March 26, 1915, the New York Court of Appeals handed down its decision. Only seven years had passed since the adverse verdict in the Williams case. Now the court overruled its earlier decision. It specifically based its opinion on the new facts brought to its attention.

In view of the incomplete manner in which the important question underlying this statute . . . was presented to us in the Williams case (said the court) we ought not to regard its decision as any bar to a consideration of the present statute in the light of all the facts and arguments now presented to us . . . not only as a matter of mere presentation, but because they have been developed by study and investigation during the years which have intervened since the Williams decision was made. There is no reason why we should be reluctant to give effect to new and additional knowledge upon such a subject as this, even if it did lead us to take a different view of such a vastly important question as that of public health or disease than formerly prevailed.

Mrs. Kelley hailed this decision, as she had the reversal of the first Ritchie decision in Illinois, with the utmost satisfaction. A similar success was now to be expected in the appeal of the Schweinler Press case to the U. S. Supreme Court. Unfortunately, owing to a defect in the legal record, the appeal was not allowed. It was not until eight years later, in 1924, in the New York Radice case, that the issue of night work for women was passed upon by the U. S. Supreme Court which unanimously upheld the New York law. The case was ably argued by Irving Goldsmith, assistant attorney general of New York, who also presented to the court the summary of "facts of knowledge" originally submitted to the New York Court of Appeals in the Schweinler Press case of 1914, revised and brought down to date.

Finally we come to a series of cases concerned with a different set of laws. I have already described Mrs. Kelley's growing conviction of the primacy of adequate wages as basic to the well being of wage earners. I have told how she returned from the International Meeting of Consumers Leagues in 1908, excited about the new minimum wage doctrine. After the initial act passed by Massachusetts in 1912, eight other states enacted minimum wage laws in 1913.

The first of these acts to be put into effect was that of Oregon. In September, 1913, the Oregon Industrial Welfare Commission, after conferences composed, as required by law, of representatives of employers, of the workers, and of the general public, promulgated its first orders. Among these, a minimum weekly wage of $8.64 was fixed for women employed in factories in the city of Portland. A manufacturer of boxes, F. C. Stettler, applied for an injunction to restrain the commission from enforcing its order. A lower court denied the application, upholding the law, and the case was carried on appeal to the Supreme Court of Oregon.

Here was a chance to bring before a state court of last resort the human implications of this new measure. Mr. Brandeis was invited to cooperate with the Oregon commission and submitted a brief of two hundred pages, which we prepared to show the world's experience with women's wages: the evil effects of low wages, and the benefits of an adequate wage from the physical, economic, and moral standpoints.

On March 17, 1914, the Supreme Court of Oregon, in a decision momentous for the future, upheld the validity of the Industrial Welfare Commission's rulings. Nine months later, Mr. Brandeis and the attorney general of Oregon argued the case, *Stettler* v. *O'Hara*, before the U. S. Supreme Court. Mrs. Kelley's satisfaction was intense in hearing Mr. Brandeis expound the facts: wages were not a purely private concern any more than hours of labor are private; on the contrary, the terms of the wage contract touch the public welfare at a hundred points and lead, when too low, to public evils threatening to the state. These commonplace truths were not then as self-evident as they have since become.

Judge William Hitz, of the District of Columbia Supreme Court, also heard Mr. Brandeis that day and recorded his impression in a letter to his friend Felix Frankfurter: "I have just heard Mr. Brandeis make one of the greatest arguments I have ever listened to. . . . He spoke on the minimum wage cases in the Supreme Court, and the reception which he wrested from that citadel of the past was very moving and impressive to one who knows the Court. . . . When Brandeis began to speak, the Court showed all the inertia and elemental hostility which courts cherish for a new thought, or a new right or even a new remedy for an old wrong, but he visibly lifted all this burden, and without orationizing or chewing of the rag he reached them all."

This appraisal by a friend of minimum wage was apparently a little too optimistic, for a long silence followed. Over a year passed and no decision was rendered by the Supreme Court in *Stettler* v. *O'Hara*. The fate of minimum wage laws in eleven states hung in the balance.

We surmised that the court was divided, that a majority could not be found to accept legal regulation of wages as a proper exercise of the state's police power. The judges apparently felt that government interference with wages went far beyond government interference with hours. Mrs. Kelley waited for the court's decision with mounting indignation:

"Whatever the final decision may be, the court's delay has caused incalculable injury to wage earning women in this country," she wrote. "The cost of living has steadily risen everywhere, and the need for minimum wage commissions has been for diverse reasons greater than ever before."

The prospect was somber, and somber was Mrs. Kelley's mood. Again in advance of her time, she was evolving in 1916 some of the possible cures which became, twenty years later, centers of controversy. If the court should decide that under the federal Constitution states could not establish the "floor beneath wages," the National Consumers League, she felt, would be confronted with the tremendous task of undertaking to change the Constitution. For she believed that a democratic, industrial republic could not go on forever "with increasing masses of people unable by honest work to live in health and frugal decency." She thought it might be necessary, if the case were decided adversely, to consider whether the Supreme Court itself and its powers and duties ought to be modified. Perhaps a unanimous vote (or unanimity except for a single written dissenting opinion) should be required to invalidate a state law—especially a law approved by referendum vote of the people and upheld by the state's own supreme court.

Meanwhile, in February, 1916, Mr. Brandeis was appointed to the U. S. Supreme Court. With the minimum wage case still undecided, Mrs. Kelley was at liberty to express appreciation for his services as unpaid counsel for the Consumers League:

> During the nine years of Mr. Brandeis' priceless service as legal advisor of the Consumers League, no case was decided adversely in which he took part in the oral argument, or for which under his guidance the League supplied either a brief or material for the use of the state in preparing its defense of a statute.

Mrs. Kelley well recognized the wider implications of these legal victories:

> In the appointment of Mr. Brandeis to the Supreme Court, the wage earners—both men and women—have lost their great advocate. . . . Mr. Brandeis has assured to millions of women a shorter working day now and in all future. And the lasting

change that he has wrought in the manner of defending labor laws before the courts is of even greater importance. . . .

In this new manner of presenting labor cases, and in the attitude of the courts towards them, are involved life and death, health and welfare for millions of obscure toilers in the long future of our industrial evolution. In it is involved, also, in great measure the hope of peaceful change from industrial chaos, as our generation has known and suffered it, to the orderly industrial life of the future.[5]

During the six months before his appointment to the U. S. Supreme Court, Mr. Brandeis and I had been working on another brief, in some respects wider in scope than any previous one. This was in defense of Oregon's new ten-hour law, passed in 1913, which covered men as well as women in manufacturing establishments. The Oregon Supreme Court upheld this act in 1914, and this decision, too, was appealed to the U. S. Supreme Court, in the case of *Bunting* v. *Oregon*. Special arguments as to the injury to women from excessive hours were, of course, not germane in the Bunting case. It was necessary to show a similar injury to adult men. Among other sources, we drew on recent British studies of the effect of long hours on output, health, and safety of men and women employed in war plants in the early years of the First World War. These studies showed that England recognized even in wartime the bad effects of long-continued overtime and excessive hours of work.

When Mr. Brandeis was appointed to the Supreme Court, he naturally withdrew from the Bunting case. He recommended Felix Frankfurter, then a professor of the Harvard Law School, as his successor as counsel for the Consumers League. Mr. Frankfurter directed the completion of the brief and appeared with the attorney general of Oregon in April, 1916, in defense of the ten-hour law.

Late in 1916 the Supreme Court asked for reargument in both these Oregon cases—*Stettler* v. *O'Hara* and *Bunting* v. *Oregon*—involving two still undecided issues: the consti-

⁵ National Consumers League, Report for 1916.

tutionality of minimum wage laws for women, and maximum hour laws for men. Probably because there had been a previous oral argument in each case, the state of Oregon waived its right to further argument and without notice to us in the Consumers League filed a request to submit these two important issues on printed briefs. Mrs. Kelley and I were horror-stricken. In all our previous experience the oral presentation had proved its great value. The judges had listened attentively, they had asked questions, and the arguments of opposing counsel had been answered. We were convinced that the oral argument had greatly helped to secure the unbroken line of favorable decisions. Were these benefits all to be lost? We had the greatest confidence in Mr. Frankfurter, who had immersed himself in the scientific and social evidence. We knew he would make an outstanding argument. But we could do nothing.

Fortunately, the Supreme Court itself wanted these matters presented orally and set them down for reargument one after the other in January, 1917. Mr. Frankfurter appeared alone on behalf of the state of Oregon in both cases.

Mrs. Kelley reported that "In both the ten-hour and the minimum wage case, Mr. Frankfurter's argument was particularly forcible in its close correlation of the industrial facts and the purely legal argument concerning the meaning of due process of law." She expressed her appreciation of "his continuous work and interest, so unstintingly given." Such continuous work and interest, unstintingly given, the Consumers League was to receive from Mr. Frankfurter until he was appointed some twenty years later to the U. S. Supreme Court.

After the reargument, the Oregon ten-hour law for men was upheld unanimously. The long fight to establish the right of the states to use their police power to regulate hours of work was finally won in 1917.

But in the minimum wage case we did not fare so well. Justice Brandeis took no part in the decision. The other eight members of the court split four to four. No opinion was written. This tie vote left in effect the decision of the Oregon Supreme Court of 1914, which had sustained the law. For the time being, the minimum wage movement was saved from complete destruction, but nothing was permanently settled, no precedent had been established. As later events proved, the conflict over minimum wage had just begun.

The battle continued for twenty years. Between 1917 and 1923, four more state supreme courts upheld their minimum wage laws. To all these states we had sent copies of the Stettler brief which was used to help defend the law. We knew that the issue must finally be settled in the U. S. Supreme Court. But it was not one of these favorable decisions which reached there. Instead, it was a case testing the law passed by Congress for the District of Columbia. This law had been contested by a hospital in the case to become famous as *Adkins* v. *Children's Hospital.* It had been upheld in the first court in the District and by a two-to-one vote at its first hearing in the District of Columbia Court of Appeals. Unfortunately, there was a rehearing; a judge ill at the first hearing was back for the second, and in November, 1922, by a two-to-one vote, the District of Columbia minimum wage law was held unconstitutional and its enforcement came to a halt. I well remember the exclamation of R. H. Tawney, an Englishman who had been connected with minimum wage work in his own country, who chanced to be in Washington at this time. "What," he cried, "isn't the constitutionality of minimum wage in this country settled *yet?* Why it is ten years since the Massachusetts law was passed! How can you do anything in the United States when the courts can hold things up like that?"

By this time I had been succeeded on the Consumers League staff by Mary W. Dewson.[6] It was she who had

---

[6] I had in 1919 accepted the position of secretary to a national committee for the study of nursing and nursing education financed by the Rockefeller Foundation.

worked with Mrs. Evans in Massachusetts in 1911 for the first American commission to study the need for minimum wage protection for women workers. Now she collaborated with Mr. Frankfurter in preparing a brief in the Adkins case, and he joined in the oral argument both in the Court of Appeals of the District and in the U. S. Supreme Court. There had been changes in the court since the four-to-four tie in 1917. Again Justice Brandeis did not participate, partly perhaps because his daughter Elizabeth was secretary of the District of Columbia Minimum Wage Board. But even with his vote we could not have won. The law was held unconstitutional by a five-to-three vote.[7] This time the Brandeis type of brief apparently did not impress the majority. Justice Sutherland, who wrote the majority opinion, remarked: "We have been furnished with a large number of printed opinions approving the policy of the minimum wage, and our own reading has disclosed a large number to the contrary. These are all proper enough for the consideration of law-making bodies . . . but they reflect no legitimate light upon the question of its [the law's] validity."

Justice Holmes, in his characteristic dissent, brilliantly expressed what we all felt as to the reactionary character of the opinion.

I confess that I do not understand the principle on which the power to fix a minimum for the wages of women can be denied by those who admit the power to fix a maximum for their hours of work. . . . *Muller* v. *Oregon,* I take it, is as good law today as it was in 1908. It will need more than the Nineteenth Amendment to convince me that there are no differences between men and women, or that legislation cannot take those differences into account. I should not hesitate to take them into account if I thought it necessary to sustain this Act. . . . But after *Bunting* v. *Oregon* . . . I had supposed that it was not necessary, and that *Lochner* v. *New York* . . . would be allowed a deserved repose.

Mrs. Kelley turned to good account her indignation at

---

[7] *Adkins* v. *Children's Hospital,* 261 U. S. 525 (1923).

the Adkins decision. She collected and had published a little volume of comment by the legal profession. "It is a volume modest and inexpensive," she wrote, "yet massive and weighty as an authority, consisting of seventeen contributions from members of the faculties of a dozen universities and law schools to law publications of the highest standing." The introduction was by Dean Roscoe Pound of Harvard.

In spite of this disastrous setback, Mrs. Kelley refused to accept it as final. It yet remained to be seen how the U. S. Supreme Court would deal with a state minimum wage law as distinguished from the act for the District. Never would she yield to pessimism or inaction while any road remained open. In her report for 1924 she declared:

"Timid friends who spread statements that the program of work for minimum wage laws is stopped, are as injurious to wage-earning women as active enemies. For in this land of volatile minds and unlimited propaganda, every movement for women and youth in industry must be continuous at all costs, and ours," she concluded in defiance, "is *continuous*. There is nothing final in the present status. Courts change. Decisions also change with time, though not without long and sustained effort."

Meanwhile, the minimum wage laws were still being challenged in state courts. Through Mrs. Catherine Edson, the able woman member of the California Industrial Welfare Commission, the National Consumers League was asked to help defend the minimum wage rulings of California. A new brief was prepared by Miss Dewson and Mr. Frankfurter, showing the beneficial working of the rates there established. At the latter's suggestion, the brief was submitted to the court on behalf of about a dozen influential organizations of women. Unfortunately, this case was technically defective and failed to be passed upon by the court at all.

In 1925, to our chagrin, a state law of Arizona was brought before the U. S. Supreme Court. The law was badly drawn and admitted of no strong defense. Following the District of Columbia precedent, it was held invalid, Justice Brandeis dissenting. This, then, seemed final. No good purpose would be served by bringing any other minimum wage law before the court.

Nothing was left now but to urge continuous scrutiny of women's wages, and as long as mandatory minimum wage legislation was invalid, at least for the present, to further the enactment of state laws which followed the Massachusetts model. The Massachusetts law had no real teeth, no penalties. But it provided for investigation and publicity of women's wages and for the enforcement of wage rates through publication in the newspapers of the names of recalcitrant employers. "The underlying object," said Mrs. Kelley, "was to give notice to one and all that we have not gone to sleep, that we have not abandoned the idea, that here is a going concern, here is Massachusetts turning the light on wages." Though totally inadequate as a final solution, this measure might, meantime, keep the subject to the fore.

At the same time, Mrs. Kelley turned to what she had come to see as the more fundamental task. The Adkins decision had brought to a head long standing indignation at the nullifying of labor laws by judicial pronouncement. What could be done to check this trend? In April, 1923, ten days after the minimum wage case had been decided by the Supreme Court, Mrs. Kelley called a conference of interested organizations and individuals to consider "the situation created by the Adkins decision."

"The effort to modernize the United States Supreme Court comes to us by default," she wrote to her staunch supporter, Myrta Jones. "No one tackles it, and one of our fields of work is barred so far as its major effectiveness is concerned until the Court is modernized." The National Consumers League proposed to get the best obtainable advice as to possible action from lawyers of progressive views and members of law faculties. "With wise, patient John Commons getting twenty legal opinions as to modernizing before he names his Committee, results are ahead if he and I both live," Mrs. Kelley concluded.

She thereupon plunged into a voluminous correspondence with such men as Felix Frankfurter, Roscoe Pound, Thomas Reed Powell, William Gorham Rice, Zechariah Chafee, Robert Szold, Bernard Shientag, Walker Nellis, Ernst Freund, Newton Baker, Edward Costigan, and others.

Many suggestions for modernizing the courts were canvassed: a constitutional amendment covering one or many phases of social legislation; the requirement that the court must be unanimous when declaring a federal or state act unconstitutional, or at least have seven votes on that side; restriction of the court's power to review, by withdrawing certain specific categories subject to the "due process" clause; enlargement of the Supreme Court; and various other remedies.

By this time, 1924, sundry bills dealing with the curtailment of judicial power in labor cases had been introduced into Congress, notably by Senators La Follette and Borah.

Mrs. Kelley's wide correspondence on this topic is notable here, particularly for her extensive exchange of letters with her old friend Charles F. Amidon, of the Federal District Court in North Dakota. Judge Amidon, a man of wide vision, was an outstanding progressive among his judicial brethren, and he took occasion in these letters to pay generous tribute to Mrs. Kelley's influence on his thinking. "The conversations we had together in our home while you were here," he wrote, "have been one of the liberalizing forces in my life. . . . During the last twelve or fifteen years of my active work on the bench I never decided a lawsuit without immersing myself at first hand with the life out of which it arose. You were one of the persons who got that lesson home in my life."

Judge Amidon recognized the consequences of the long, protracted fights to establish the constitutionality of hour and wage laws. "How can there be any respect," he wrote, "when every important statute after it is enacted and approved has to go through all our wilderness wandering of litigation, with the power in every court from a justice of the peace to the Supreme Court of the United States to suspend its force, and with the chance about equal in the end that it will finally be held unconstitutional?"

Mrs. Kelley, on her part, rated Judge Amidon's proposals as supremely important in this far-ranging discussion of means. "It is your letters which transformed the subject of action . . . from my mere hobby (so it had been held) to *the* burning question confronting the National Consumers League for as long a time as may be necessary to restore government by the people to this Republic."

In the end, nothing came of all this travail in the twenties, owing largely to the failure to come to agreement upon the best solution.

To complete the record, however, I give the final acts of the minimum wage drama, which came after Mrs. Kelley's death. In 1933, we of the Consumers League decided to make a new effort to re-establish this method of melioration for working women. The depression, with its lowering of wages almost to the vanishing point, once more threw into high relief the desperate need for government action. A new minimum wage bill was drafted by Mr. Frankfurter and by Mr. Benjamin V. Cohen, whose unusual ability in bill drafting was then for the first time enlisted by us. This bill was designed to meet the requirements laid down by Justice Sutherland's opinion in the District of Columbia case. It was promptly introduced into the legislatures of eight states, and within a few months was passed in six states.

To secure the best possible test we persuaded other states to delay action and succeeded in having appealed to Washington a case involving the new minimum wage law of New York.

The law was defended by the state solicitor general, Mr.

Henry Epstein, with an able economic brief prepared by the state Labor Department under Frieda S. Miller, the industrial commissioner. For the first time the National Consumers League was balked in its effort to obtain an invitation for eminent counsel to join the state in this crucial defense, on which were set the hopes of the other states besides New York, which had in such rapid succession passed our Standard Minimum Wage Act.[8] The value of having these other states represented to show the national implications of the case was self-evident. But for reasons best known to himself, the responsible official, Attorney General John M. Bennett of New York, refused to extend such an invitation to any lawyer, however eminent. Fortunately, Dean Acheson, then a practicing lawyer in Washington, generously agreed to appear as *amicus curiae* in the oral argument and by brief, to present the case for the other states.

But our efforts were in vain. By a vote of five to four in June, 1936, the court once more declared a minimum wage statute invalid, though the greatest pains had been taken to meet the legalistic objections raised in 1923.[9] This adverse decision climaxed a series in which the Supreme Court had held various New Deal laws unconstitutional. But here it was a state not a federal law which the court held invalid. Thus it maintained the barrier against both kinds of government action to remedy economic ills. Franklin D. Roosevelt declared the court was still in the horse-and-buggy era. The Consumers League was active in attempts to frame a constitutional amendment. The President proposed his "court packing plan." Since none of this is Mrs. Kelley's story, it may suffice to say that fortunately in the next year, 1937, another minimum wage case—this time from the state of Washington—reached the U. S. Supreme Court. The court overruled its previous decisions. By the narrow margin of a

---

[8] These states were Connecticut, Illinois, Massachusetts, New Hampshire, New Jersey, and Rhode Island.

[9] *Morehead* v. *New York ex rel. Tipaldo*, 298 U. S. 587 (1936).

five-to-four vote, minimum wage laws were finally upheld.[10]
Those of us who had worked so long with Mrs. Kelley re-
called her shrewd comment in 1911, "But is the trouble
really in the Constitution? Or is it in the judges?"

---

[10] *West Coast Hotel Co.* v. *Parrish*, 300 U. S. 379 (1937).

Chapter 15

Mrs. Kelley Opposes the Woman's Party

During the twenties, Florence Kelley found herself confronting a new danger to the cause which she had made her own: the effort to counterbalance by law the special handicaps faced by girls and women in life's struggle, especially in the industrial arena. This new danger, she felt, derived from the Woman's Party organized in 1921 to demand equality with men for women through a federal constitutional amendment.

She was for many years vice-president of the National Woman Suffrage Association and an active worker in the suffrage cause. She had even joined the first Woman's Party, set up to push for suffrage more militantly than the old suffrage association. She thought that this group, younger and more aggressive than the older suffrage leaders, would, as she whimsically put it, "galvanize into action from lifelong effort the old-line 'suffs.'" She gave the new group credit for a brilliant performance in the closing phases of the suffrage campaign.

But immediately after the vote was won in 1920, the Woman's Party disbanded and a new organization with the same name was formed. The old party had secured equal suffrage through an amendment to the federal Constitution; the new party was established to seek by the same method to secure equal rights for women in all other respects. With the general objectives of the proposed amendment Florence Kelley was naturally in full accord. "All modern minded people desire, of course," she wrote, "that women should have full political equality and be free from the exclusions from the bench, the bar, the pulpit, the highest ranges of the teachers' profession and of the civil service. Obviously, all elective and appointive offices should be open to women and they should have every opportunity for jury duty and the right to equal guardianship of their children." [1]

Moreover, it was tempting at first sight to secure all this at one time. A second constitutional amendment to supplement the suffrage amendment looked like a short-cut to secure for women all the rights (beyond suffrage) to which, by temperament, training, and experience, Mrs. Kelley was deeply committed. But what else might it do at the same time? Complete equality with men before the law—did the wage earning girls and women for whom she had worked all her life really want that? What would the amendment do to women's hour laws, night work laws, minimum wage laws, which the Consumers League had won from legislatures and defended in the courts? At first the leaders of the Woman's Party declared that in the wording of the amendment such legislation might be specifically exempted from the general declaration of equal rights. Mrs. Kelley was made a member of an advisory committee, and various wordings were submitted to her for criticism.[2]

"I can think of few things more painful than having to

---

[1] The *Survey*, March 5, 1921, p. 827.

[2] The exact wording of the proposed amendment was discussed for a long time and has come through various forms. In recent sessions it has read: "Equality of rights under the law shall not be denied or abridged by the United States or by any state on account of sex." The amendment has been introduced in Congress year after year, but it has not been passed by either House. (Except in 1950 by the Senate and then only after the addition of a proviso passed by the Senate which would virtually nullify its effect. Jt. Res. 25, 81st Congress, January 25, 1950.)

oppose a measure that you are advocating," Mrs. Kelley wrote to her dear friend and former fellow worker, Maud Younger, of California, an influential member of the Woman's Party, who sent alternative forms of the bill. Maud Younger had been one of our most valuable allies in getting enacted by Congress the eight-hour law of 1912 for women employed in the District of Columbia. Six months after her first letter, Mrs. Kelley had come to a decision. Painful as it was to be obliged to oppose her, she wrote Maud, "Your present activities run counter to my continuous efforts of more than five and thirty years, and I cannot stand idly by. . . . They are prudent advisors who inform you that 'so far as one can predict,' your amendment will not be interpreted as touching protective legislation for women."

In fact, those of us who believed in special labor legislation for women soon realized that the leaders of the Woman's Party actually wanted such legislation destroyed. In our discussions with them they would declare that a maximum hour law or a minimum wage law which applied to women but not to men was bound to hurt women more than it could possibly help them.

A final effort was made to reach a compromise. On December 4, 1921, Mrs. Kelley, for the National Consumers League; Miss Ethel Smith, for the National Women's Trade Union League; Mrs. Maud Wood Park, for the National League of Women Voters; and representatives of the General Federation of Women's Clubs and of the Young Women's Christian Association met for two hours with Miss Paul and two members of the board of the Woman's Party, but to no effect. Following this conference, the board of directors of the National Consumers League, on motion of Larue Brown, a former assistant U. S. attorney-general, voted definitely to oppose the amendment.

Mrs. Kelley reluctantly took up the cudgel against what she called "topsy-turvy feminism." For the remaining ten years of her life she made opposition to the so-called "equal rights" amendment a regular part of Consumers League work, seeing the proposal as a major threat to women's labor laws, to maternity aid, mothers' pensions, and other legislative protection for women. In a voluminous correspondence, a stream of articles, popular and technical, and in conferences and meetings, she sought to clarify the issue. She declared that the members of the Woman's Party were a highly articulate minority of professional women, ignorant of the real needs of their wage earning sisters. She charged that they were actually making common cause with, or allowing themselves to be used by, exploiting employers. She pointed to legislative hearings at which employers and Woman's Party representatives appeared together to push blanket "equality" laws or to oppose special laws for women.

"Will the new party," she asked, "failing to discriminate between the needs of the professional group and those of the wage earning multitude, become the effective tool of exploiting employers who maintain and seek to prolong these industrial evils?"

Mrs. Kelley made in those early years the two major arguments against the "equal rights" amendment which remain the basic objections to this method of achieving women's rights. First, she declared that women cannot achieve true equality with men by securing identity of treatment under the law. Because women are not identical with men they have certain different problems and need certain different legal remedies. Second, she saw that blanket action through a constitutional amendment would involve an interminable series of court decisions to determine what laws the amendment would permit or invalidate. Mrs. Kelley, who had spent a lifetime battling court interpretations of the "due process" clause of the Fourteenth Amendment, was especially fitted to recognize this danger in a new broad general amendment.

Identity of treatment, Mrs. Kelley pointed out, would bring to wage earning women not bread but a stone. At one stroke it would deprive them of safeguards painfully won by long struggle. The amendment, she said, would prevent working women from obtaining or retaining what men could and did obtain for themselves: legislation to meet their own specific needs and desires. She pointed out, for instance, that men in many mining states had obtained for themselves the eight-hour day by law, even changing state constitutions to do so. Other special legislation obtained by men were the laws "safeguarding those (commonly known as sand hogs) who work in tunnels under rivers and harbors, and bills [i.e., laws] applying to men in the train service of railroads and on scaffolds in the building trades. Women obviously do not work in mines and tunnels and on scaffolds. They form no part of train crews under the full crew laws. Their oldest, most wide-spread and most insistent demands have been for seats, for more adequate wages, and short, firmly regulated working hours." [3]

But when it came to obtaining laws providing these more ordinary safeguards for women, the Woman's Party said *no*.

Men, Mrs. Kelley further pointed out, could and did obtain shorter hours and better wages through collective bargaining by their unions. Women needed laws to counterbalance their special handicaps in bargaining power, handicaps such as the greater youth of girls and women in industry as compared with men, their inexperience, their greater instability because of prospective marriage, their physical handicaps. "The vast majority of women wage-earners are between the ages of sixteen and twenty-five years. They are not the material of which militant trade unions are formed. Their wages are too small to supply war chests for strikes. Their accumulated experience is too slight for the successful conduct of more than an occasional brief walkout. These

[3] *Good Housekeeping*, March, 1924, p. 165.

facts common to all industrial countries compel protective legislation for women." [4]

Mrs. Kelley summed up in a paragraph the differentiation of method used by men and women in obtaining relief from oppressive conditions: "Whenever union men feel no need of laws, well and good. No one wishes to interfere with them any more than professional women are interfered with by labor legislation. . . . Women in general get their shorter day by law and men by negotiation backed when necessary by strikes. Both are legal." [5]

But under the "equal rights" amendment, working women would be able to have their hours and working conditions regulated by law only if men wanted to have the *same* legislation. The Woman's Party opposed any and all laws special to women. "This would be a new subjection of wage-earning women to wage-earning men," declared Mrs. Kelley, "and to that subjection we are opposed on principle and in practice. . . . On this subject we are immovable."

Women claimed not *identity*, but equality of treatment. "The acid test of their quality," declared Mrs. Kelley, was the pragmatic test: *"the extent to which they benefit from it."* [6]

Other special measures for women, besides the labor laws, were threatened. For example, the laws providing for widows' pensions were clearly discriminations for women. What would happen to these laws? And would husbands need to continue to support their wives, under the proposed amendment? Could deserting husbands be brought back and compelled to provide for wife and child? What would happen to the age of consent, and to penalties for seduction, rape, and violations of the Mann Act. Such penalties obviously applied to men alone.

---

[4] "Should Women Be Treated Identically with Men by the Law?" *American Review*, March-April, 1923.

[5] *Good Housekeeping*, March, 1924, p. 165.

[6] "Should Women Be Treated Identically with Men by the Law?" *American Review*, March-April, 1923.

Above all, what would become of the federal Maternity and Infancy Act which provided aid to the states for maternity care? To this measure Florence Kelley was devoting a substantial portion of her time and an intensity of feeling perhaps unequaled in any other phase of her work. Would this beneficent act, too, go down in the general ruin?

One of Mrs. Kelley's objections to the "equal rights" amendment was the certainty that it would need long, protracted interpretation by the courts before any one could know what its consequences would be. Sometimes its proponents argued that all special laws which were actually beneficial to women would be sustained as constitutional under the amendment. But who would decide which laws were beneficial? The best constitutional lawyers agreed with Mrs. Kelley that nobody could say what the courts would do.

Every amendment to the Constitution is a pig in a poke. No one now living can foretell what the effects of the one proposed would be. Clear and simple as its words look, they are ambiguous . . . how ambiguous may be seen from the diametrically opposed views about their meaning held by Miss Dock and myself, friends for a quarter century. The all-important point is not what Miss Dock hopes, nor what I fear. The all-important point is that the meaning of the Equal Rights amendment depends on the United States Supreme Court. . . . The Supreme Court has . . . held unconstitutional two federal child labor laws and a minimum wage law.

In somewhat more parliamentary language, she wrote to Senator Curtis of Kansas, "To these numerous weighty questions there is but one final and convincing answer, the voice of the United States Supreme Court. Is it not the greatest objection to the amendment that it will, if enacted, clog the Courts, from the magistrates' sessions to the Supreme Bench, for many years to come?"

In this matter Mrs. Kelley took counsel with eminent lawyers. She consulted, among others, Newton Baker who was president of the Consumers League, and Dean Roscoe

Pound and Felix Frankfurter of the Harvard Law School. The tenor of the replies is indicated by Mr. Baker, "How can anyone venture to take such a risk? I had had in my mind only industrial legislation as I formulated my own objections to the amendment, but the whole realm of domestic relations and all the accomplishments of the last 25 or 50 years in bettering the position of women and children seems to me to be at stake and I dread to think of the possibility of success for an amendment which will re-open so many settled questions and cause so much perilous litigation."

Mrs. Kelley foresaw that the fight to prevent enactment of the amendment would be a long one. To one correspondent she wrote, "We shall have to oppose Alice Paul and her followers for years to come." In similar vein, she closed a letter to Dean Pound with the following: "Assuring you that I should not be trespassing on your interest in the peaceful development of industry under the law, if there were not in plain sight an immediate campaign that will be carried on until the leaders of the Woman's Party all die of old age. . . ."

Florence Kelley's opposition to the "equal rights" amendment was never merely negative. On the contrary, the proposal intensified her fighting desire to obtain for women specific measures to end specific discriminations. As she said, "The ballot is our most recently acquired instrument of choice and change. With it, statutes can be fitted precisely and skillfully to the needs of every group in the community as each need is clearly recognized." By temperament she was essentially an impatient person. Yet she had spent her life in working to improve the lot of wage earning women and children, one step at a time, one state at a time, through specific measures.

Unfortunately, the young women in the Woman's Party lacked her patience and derided her methods. They were probably deluded by what they thought was their quick victory in winning the vote for women. They failed to appreciate that their success was but the culmination of the long, patient educational campaign of several generations of woman suffragists, beginning in the days when Florence Kelley's father addressed suffrage conventions in the seventies. They thought it would be easy (and desirable) to wipe out all remaining discrimination against women in one fell swoop. Most of the discriminations in the laws of the land against women which the Woman's Party denounced—with Mrs. Kelley agreeing—have in the last twenty-five years been eliminated by specific legislation. The handicaps to women that remain are mostly matters of custom and tradition; they are social, not legal, barriers.

Since the twenties the need for special labor laws for women has diminished for three reasons: first, the courts have at last accepted as constitutional the hour and wage laws for men. Second, and even more important, the union labor movement now recognizes the need for legislative protection of men workers as well as women—witness the support of the federal wage-hour law by both the Congress of Industrial Organization and the American Federation of Labor. Third, the growing union movement has recently included women far more effectively than in Mrs. Kelley's day. The combination of these three changes means that if the "equal rights" amendment should be adopted it would probably do far less harm than it would have done in the twenties.

Still, many of us believe that Mrs. Kelley's basic argument remains valid. Blanket action, positive or negative, is rarely desirable in the complicated field of government. Laws should be carefully drawn, designed to meet specific situations. A general "equal rights" pronouncement in the federal Constitution is no solution to the problems of women in the modern industrial world.

Chapter 16

The Dial-Painters' Story

Mrs. Kelley was perplexed and horrified as she listened to Katherine Wiley's story. Miss Wiley was secretary of the New Jersey Consumers League, and this was a day in 1924 when she had come over to the National League office in New York to see Mrs. Kelley. Such a visit was not unusual; Miss Wiley often came over to consult on issues and policies and, like all Consumers League workers, to gain fresh impetus and courage from Mrs. Kelley.

But on this particular day, Miss Wiley had a fantastic, macabre story to tell. The Board of Health of Orange County had asked Miss Wiley, as secretary of an organization interested in working girls, to look into a peculiar coincidence— the sickness and death of a number of girls employed at the plant of the U. S. Radium Corporation in Newark, New Jersey. This request was not unprecedented. The New Jersey League, like those in other states, was small in numbers but influential out of all proportion to its size. It was known as a group with accurate knowledge of industrial matters and the courage to attack abuses. The Orange County Board of Health might properly concern itself about what was happening in the Radium Corporation plant. Significantly, it turned to the Consumers League—a small, private, voluntary organization—to look into the situation.

Katherine Wiley had accepted the assignment and gone to work. She found that four girls had died and that eight others were desperately sick. The cause of death was stated as anemia and necrosis of the jaw. She visited the girls who were ill and the families of those who had died. The girls had all worked in the factory, painting watch dials with luminous paint; otherwise they had nothing in common. In general, she thought the hygienic conditions in the factory good, and in this, the Labor Department, which was also investigating the matter, agreed. But in painting with luminous paint, the girls repeatedly pointed their brushes with their lips. Was there anything in the paint which might account for the illness which had been fatal in four cases? The girls had had repeated jaw operations. She called on the dentists who had treated them and found them baffled by the unexpectedly bad results following extraction of teeth. The symptoms had some resemblance to the dreaded "phossy jaw" disease which had been notorious in the early years of the century and which had led to the federal tax ending the use of phosphorus in the manufacture of matches. But the chemist of the New Jersey Department of Labor reported no phosphorus in the luminous paint. It was a mixture of zinc oxide and radium or mesothorium. In 1924 the danger of these chemicals was not realized. This method of illuminating watch dials had been introduced in this country in 1913 and was used for a decade before its effects came to light.

Now Miss Wiley and Mrs. Kelley suspected the presence of a new and hideous industrial poison. What could they do? "It is all so new and insidious—one is dead or crippled before it is discovered to be coming," said Miss Wiley. Mrs. Kelley had for years wished to include a study of industrial diseases among women as part of the work of the Consumers League. She had followed Dr. Alice Hamilton's pioneering work with the keenest interest. In fact, we had set up a special committee on industrial diseases in 1917 after Dr. Hamilton's investigations had disclosed TNT poisoning in munitions plants. But by 1924 this committee had lapsed. The story of the dial painters aroused Mrs. Kelley anew. The League must do something.

Meanwhile, unknown to the Consumers League, from two separate sources came a tentative answer to the mystery of the dial-painters' disease. The first medical comment in this country appeared in September, 1924, in a footnote to an article on oral surgery by Dr. Theodore Blum. He stated that he had, in the fall of 1923, observed a case "somewhat similar to phosphorus necrosis [of the jaw] which, however, was caused by some radioactive substance used in the manufacturing of luminous dials for watches." [1] At the time, this statement went unnoticed.

Secondly, unknown to anyone except the parties concerned, the Harvard School of Public Health had, at the request of the U. S. Radium Corporation, investigated the dial-painting process and found evidence of radium poisoning. Dr. Cecil K. Drinker and his associates at Harvard, after a two-month investigation, reported to the corporation in June, 1924, that the girls engaged in dial painting were absorbing minute quantities of radium by "pointing" the brushes with their lips. Moreover, minute particles of radium had been found in the dust in the workroom which might be absorbed through the lungs.

Obviously this report by the Harvard investigators was a scientific document of the greatest importance, not only to remedy conditions in this plant but to acquaint other manufacturers, using the same radium formula, with its toxicity and potentially lethal effects. Science and humanity alike demanded immediate publication of this report. But the U. S. Radium Corporation, having commissioned and paid for the investigation, now refused permission to publish. The facts, naturally, reflected on the plant; they might well serve

---

[1] Theodore Blum, "Osteomyelitis of the Mandible and Maxilla," *Journal of the American Dental Association*, September, 1924, p. 802.

as a basis for damage suits. Rumors of the investigation had leaked out, but the report was resolutely suppressed.

Since Mrs. Kelley and Miss Wiley could not secure publication of the results of the Harvard investigation, they decided to get someone else with standing to investigate the situation, and make public what was found. Miss Wiley called on Dr. Frederick Hoffman, the well-known statistician of the Prudential Life Insurance Company. Dr. Hoffman was immediately struck by the coincidence of four deaths and the illness of eight other girls from similar causes, all of them having worked at one time or other at the same plant. This mortality and morbidity could not be mere coincidence. Dr. Hoffman decided to comply with the suggestion of the Consumers League that he should make his own investigation by calling upon the attending doctors, dentists, or others who might be in a position to aid what he called rather a "fact-finding process than a technical investigation for which I would not be qualified." [2]

Dr. Hoffman read his report at the meeting of the American Medical Association in May, 1925. It showed that the Radium Corporation, a year after receiving the report of the Harvard investigation, was disclaiming all responsibility. "In correspondence with the company concerned," said Dr. Hoffman, "I learned that it had, of course, become aware of the insinuations made from time to time that work in the plant was injurious to health, but it had been unable to trace the affections reported to any causative factor of which it could take cognizance. . . . I was informed that technically the opinion seemed to be that the minute quantity of radium introduced into the mouth could not possibly have caused the amount of damage elsewhere indicated."

[2] "Radium (mesothorium) Necrosis," *Journal of the American Medical Association*, September 26, 1925, p. 961: "The facts of the situation were first brought to my attention by the Executive Secretary of the New Jersey Consumers League with the request that I investigate the circumstances and contribute the results of my research towards a possible solution of a serious industrial disease problem."

Dr. Hoffman was not impressed by this disclaimer. He came out flatly with the "very obvious fact and conclusion" that "we are here dealing with an entirely new occupational affection:" It should, he said, be scientifically studied and brought under the scope of Workmen's Compensation for Industrial Diseases. While few women were working at the Newark plant at this time, hundreds had been employed between 1913 and 1923.

The lid was now off. Newspaper items followed publication of the Hoffman report. Secrecy being no longer of any avail, the Harvard investigation was finally published in August, 1925.[3] Even the lay reader could understand why the U. S. Radium Corporation had been reluctant to have these objective findings published. The report stated that: "Dust samples collected in the workroom from various locations and from chairs not used by the workers were all luminous in the dark room. Their hair, faces, hands, arms, necks, the dresses, the underclothes, even the corsets of the dial painters were luminous. One of the girls showed luminous spots on her legs and thighs. The back of another was luminuous almost to the waist. . . . This we think is evidence that the powdered base was being carried in suspension about the paint room and even beyond its confines."

An accepted test of overexposure to radium or X-rays, stated the Harvard investigation, is any fogging of a sealed dental film within two weeks. But here "films in the painting room showed distinct fogging at the end of two or three days."

Also, exposure to radium in excessive amounts was shown, the investigators held, by the blood count of twenty-two persons examined. "The significance of these findings is that no blood was entirely normal and that characteristics of exposure in excessive amounts appeared in many of the blood films examined."

---

[3] William B. Castle, Katherine R. Drinker, and Cecil K. Drinker, "Necrosis of the Jaw in Radium Workers," *Journal of Industrial Hygiene*, August, 1925, p. 373.

While exceedingly cautious in drawing inferences from these findings, the investigators concluded: "It seems necessary, therefore, to consider that the cases described have been due to radium. This is not finally proved, but since the remedial measures proposed are of general as well as special import, it is felt that the safest course at the present time is to treat the situation in this light."

Two months after the Harvard report was finally published, the first positive proof of death by radium poisoning in a dial painter was established. Dr. Harrison S. Martland, chief medical examiner (coroner) of Essex County, New Jersey, reported autopsy findings in the case of a young woman who had worked at painting dials for eight years (1917-25).[4] Since 1923, on instructions from the factory management, she had stopped pointing her brushes with her lips innumerable times in the day, never before having been warned of the danger of so doing.

The recent report by Hoffman [writes Dr. Martland] makes it necessary for us to report our unfinished observations on the danger of the accumulation of radioactive substances in the body and their effect. . . . We feel we have proved by the demonstration and measurement of radioactive substances in the body during life, in the expired air and in the organs after death, that the anemia in this case is dependent on the ingestion, long before, of radioactive paint, and that it is caused by actual deposits in the spleen, bones and liver of radium and mesothorium with their decayed products. For the foregoing reasons we have designated this anemia as a "rapid anemia of the pernicious type due to radioactivity." Radioactivity in the bones is very clearly shown by exposure on the dental films.

But ingestion of radium through the mouth could not have been the sole cause of radium poisoning. As if grimly to point the moral, another victim died in May, 1925; he was Dr. Lehman, the Radium Corporation's chemist. Here was

---

[4] Harrison S. Martland, Philip Conlon, and Joseph P. Knef. "Some Unrecognized Dangers in the Use and Handling of Radioactive Substances," *Journal of the American Medical Association*, December 5, 1925, p. 1669.

a man who had never painted watch dials, hence had never pointed the brushes with his lips. But the nature of his work exposed him to "varying quantities of these radioactive substances in both the sealed and unsealed forms."

Dr. Martland and his associates also reported the autopsy findings in Lehman's case, concluding: "It is definitely proven that radioactive substances can get into the body by way of the lungs alone. It is definitely established that, by way of the lungs, both radium, mesothorium and the active deposit from emanations are deposited and stored in the organs." [5]

Autopsies made in New York City (where some of the patients had died) by Dr. Charles Norris, chief medical examiner, and Dr. George Gettler, toxicologist, confirmed Dr. Martland's findings.

Two years later, in 1927, came news of radium poisoning occurring in Connecticut. Necrosis of the jaw and at least three deaths were reported among women employed as dial painters by the Ingersoll Watch Company and the Waterbury Clock Company. The radium formula used for illuminating watch dials in Connecticut had been obtained from the U. S. Radium Corporation. Here, then, in three states its lethal effects had been demonstrated.

Now the lawyers followed the doctors onto the scene. In the spring of 1925, damage suits had been filed against the U. S. Radium Corporation by the families of two women who had died and by the widow of the chemist, Dr. Lehman. In 1927, suits were filed by Raymond Berry of Newark on behalf of five young women, desperately ill, who had been employed at the plant for varying periods of time.[6]

---

[5] George S. Reitter and Harrison S. Martland, "Leucopenic Anemia of the Regenerative Type due to Exposure to Radium and Mesothorium," *Journal of the American Medical Association*, August, 1926, p. 167.

[6] These victims had no rights under the New Jersey Workmen's Compensation Law because it covered only listed industrial diseases and obviously did not include this new poison in its list. Hence their only legal remedy was to sue for damages.

As late as November, 1926, the U. S. Radium Corporation was still explicitly denying that radium poisoning in its
plant was responsible for the illnesses and deaths among its
employees. In reply to a suggestion by Dr. Hoffman that
the corporation "do something" for Miss Grace Fryer, the
first of the five young women to bring suit, the corporation
(or its lawyers) replied: "We certainly sympathize with the
young lady whose condition you describe, but are somewhat
at a loss to know just what to say, since under present conditions it is rather dangerous to take a position which might
be misunderstood or tend to establish a precedent. So far
as our information goes, scientific investigations to date do
not prove that radio-activity has been the cause of some of
the conditions commonly attributed to it." [7]

Mr. Berry claimed $250,000 damages each for Miss Fryer
and four others. Lawyers for the corporation countered by
invoking the statute of limitations. By New Jersey law, suit
had to be brought within two years after suffering injury.
But these girls had no knowledge of their fatal exposure until
more than two years had passed after it occurred. No doctor
at that time so much as recognized their symptoms. It was
an unknown disease to which they had fallen victims.

"Intolerable, despicable" were the terms used by the *New
York World* of the action of the corporation in invoking the
statue of limitations against girls, one of whom had under-
gone twenty operations on her jaw following three years' employment as a dial painter. Mr. Berry appealed to the New
Jersey Court of Chancery for an injunction against the use of
the statute of limitations. A whole year passed. Over the objection of the girls' counsel, adjournment followed adjournment in the Court of Chancery. In May, 1928, while their
symptoms and disabilities grew ever more grave, Grace
Fryer and the four other complainants were still waiting for
legal settlement. They knew their fate was inescapable, the

---

[7] Quoted in an affidavit sworn to by Miss Katherine G. T. Wiley,
July 16, 1927, attached to the bill of complaint of Miss Grace Fryer.

prognosis had been negative, and death in a horrible form lay before them. What they still awaited, in May, 1928, was any reply at all from the Court of Chancery. Their right to sue for some measure of financial relief was still unanswered. "This is one of the most damnable travesties of justice that has ever come to our attention," wrote the *New York World* in savage indignation.[8]

The stalemate continued until May 30, when an unexpected move surprised us all. Federal Judge William Clark was reported in the newspapers as unofficial mediator to settle the suits out of court. On June 4, 1928, an agreement was signed by the five young women and the Radium Corporation, whereby each of the women was paid a lump sum of $10,000 and a pension of $600 a year for life.

To one of these young women the corporation was not long obliged to pay its meager pension. On December 10, 1929, Quinta Maggia MacDonald was the first of the five to die. Miss Wiley reported her death to Mrs. Kelley: "Now one more girl has passed on from this horrible disease. I went to see her at the Memorial Hospital in New York City about a month ago. She was *so* pathetic, so lovely to look at and suffering all the time. But she felt at rest mentally about her children, who are very well cared for."

To Florence Kelley, as always in her public work, the private tragedy was heartrending. "Cold-blooded murder in industry" was her word for it. But her mind was at work upon something more constructive than indignation. What could be done for the future to stop at their source such recurring costs of industry, paid for by the workers in mutilation and death? She was "haunted," as she wrote to Alice Hamilton, by the thought of other unkown victims of radium poisoning, dying or dead, undiagnosed or wrongly diagnosed. "Syphilis," "nephritis," "gangrene of the lungs," etc., had been some of the causes of death entered on the death certificates of earlier victims at the Newark plant. "Neither

[8] Editorial of May 10, 1928.

certificate gives the slightest indication of radium affections," noted Dr. Hoffman, regarding two of the deaths he was investigating.

Everyone knew that the use of illuminated dials was increasing by leaps and bounds, not only for ordinary clocks and watches but in airplanes, speedboats, and the like. Who could make a scientific study of the production of luminous objects and the necessary safeguards, if such there were, in using this lethal formula?

Mrs. Kelley consulted Dr. Alice Hamilton, who since Hull House days had become one of the foremost American authorities on industrial disease. It was Alice Hamilton who had written in 1911 the pioneer report of the Illinois Commission on Industrial Diseases, the first in the United States. I well remember how, at the International Congress of Hygiene and Demography held in Washington, D.C., in 1912 (where I read a paper on industrial fatigue), Dr. Thomas Oliver of England, author of the monumental volume *Dangerous Trades*, sought out Dr. Hamilton. He told me she was the one physician in the United States who had published research in this branch of medicine.[9] In the following years she had done further outstanding research in industrial disease. Now in 1927 Mrs. Kelley asked her: What can the Consumers League do about radium poisoning in industry?

Together the two friends worked out an answer to that question based on the study of another industrial poison, tetra-ethyl lead. Refineries had begun adding this chemical to gasoline in the early twenties to eliminate "knocking." In 1924, widespread public indigation and fear had been aroused over eleven deaths and considerable illness and insanity in certain New Jersey and Ohio plants making this new kind of gasoline. Public concern was heightened by the fear that motorists using this new gasoline might also be endangered. Public demand had led the U. S. Public Health

---

[9] This was before Dr. David L. Edsall had begun his industrial disease studies at the Massachusetts General Hospital, a landmark of later years.

Service to call a conference of the manufacturers of "leaded" gas, which drew up regulations for handling and selling the product and provided for further investigation. The *New York World* had taken the lead in publicizing the facts, and the corporations were now cooperating in enforcing safeguards.

Why not push for similar action on radium poisoning? Of course no federal agency had power to regulate the use of industrial poisons, but in the case of tetra-ethyl lead, the federal Public Health Service, despite its lack of power, had nonetheless managed to work out a solution. And Surgeon General Hugh S. Cummings had stated in an interview that an aroused public opinion had led the Public Health Service to take action. Someone must now take the lead in presenting to the surgeon general the case of radium poisoning and must prove that here too expert and public opinion alike demanded action.

As a first step, Mrs. Kelley called a small informal meeting, inviting the medical men directly involved, Drs. Martland and Norris, the chief medical examiners, respectively, of Essex County, New Jersey, and of New York City, with Dr. Hamilton as consultant. Mr. Berry, legal counsel for the five victims, was also invited. We met at the old Cosmopolitan Club on Fortieth Street in New York, spending several hours discussing the possibilities and blocking out a program.

A communication, it was agreed, should be addressed to the surgeon general, asking him to call a conference following the tetra-ethyl lead precedent. This would be signed first by Drs. Martland and Norris, reinforced by other public health men and physicians of high standing who could be quickly reached. Dr. Hamilton would draft both the letter asking for signatures and the communication to the surgeon general. She and I were to obtain the signatures in New York, New Jersey, Connecticut, Massachusetts.[10] It was fur-

---

[10] These states were chosen because the radium cases had occurred in the first three and because of the participation of the Harvard School of Public Health in Massachusetts.

ther agreed that the *New York World* be asked to back this movement with its powerful editorial support, Mrs. Kelley undertaking to explain our plan to Walter Lippmann, then chief editorial writer. Dr. Hamilton summed up the situation in her letter of June 16, 1928, asking for signatures:

When I passed through New York I had a meeting with Drs. H. S. Martland and Charles Norris and also two representatives of the Consumers League to discuss the cases of radium poisoning in women using a radioactive mixture to make luminous figures on clocks and watches. You have doubtless seen articles in medical journals and also the frequent newspaper items, telling of the fate of some of the victims. It seems that there have been so far fifteen or seventeen deaths in New Jersey and two or three in Connecticut, but in all probability the actual number is far larger, for it is only in the past three years that the diagnosis has been made. I was informed that Norris and Martland together with Gettler succeeded in having exhumed the body of a women who died five years ago, supposedly of sepsis, but they found that emanations were still being given off from her bones. They also found that no therapeutic measure will rid the bones of this radium, which seems to be resistant to everything but boiling in hydrochloric acid.

The letter to the surgeon general recited the same facts, concluding: "We feel that a study should be made of the whole problem and publicity be given to the findings. We therefore suggest, since the problem is one affecting several of the states, that you follow the procedure so successful in the investigation of tetra-ethyl lead poisoning."

The communication to Dr. Cummings was signed by twenty-three prominent medical men, the only lay signatures being those of Florence Kelley for the National Consumers League, and John B. Andrews for the American Association for Labor Legislation.[11]

The dispatch of this letter was, however, delayed for several weeks. Mrs. Kelley and I had meantime consulted with

---

[11] Separate letters to the same effect were sent to the surgeon general by the New York Academy of Medicine through its Committee on Public Health Relations, and by the New York City Commissioner of Health.

Walter Lippmann. The day we visited him in his small office high up in the dome of the old World Building was not wholly propitious for detailing our plan. The political campaign of 1928 was in full swing and just at the moment when we reached his office, Mr. Lippmann, as I recollect it, was receiving the first wires from the Democratic National Convention in Chicago. He listened to us with interest, nevertheless, and promised his full aid as soon as the letter to the surgeon general had been sent. But he counseled delay. Mrs. Kelley explained the situation in a letter to John B. Andrews:

Josephine Goldmark and I saw Mr. Lippmann, who agreed to help in every way possible, but warned us that we should injure our case if we attempted to present it publicly before July 4th, after the close of the second Presidential Convention. This we reported to the people concerned, and an agreement was reached that there should be no publicity and no communication to Dr. Cummings until notice should be given in Dr. Hamilton's name to all cooperating persons. Obviously, nothing could be so frustrating as the firing of a pop-gun by any part of the group in advance.

No pop-gun was fired, everything went as planned. The facts as recited in the letter, the distinction of its signers in their several fields, and the *New York World* editorial of July 16, 1928, echoed throughout the country.

"In many aspects the disease is surrounded by mystery which only an expert, impartial and national agency can remove. . . . Clearly, this is a task for the United States Public Health Service to take up," concluded the editorial.

The newspapers of the country took up the story. We collected four-hundred clippings from newpapers published outside New Jersey or New York. Mrs. Kelley was persuaded to go on her vacation, but from her Maine retreat she followed events with continued intensity.[12]

---

[12] The remaining details of collating the signatures sent in to Mrs. Kelley's office, informing the press after the letter to the surgeon general had been sent, etc., were left to the research secretary of the League, Marguerite M. Marsh.

Dr. Cummings had replied encouragingly to the communication of July 16. "Certainly," he wrote to Dr. Hamilton, "the names appended to your letter and to the accompanying pages should carry enough weight in industrial medicine and research to move almost anything."

He would "begin steps immediately to take proper action." But as summer passed into autumn Mrs. Kelley's anxiety began to mount. No conference had been called. Alice Hamilton had commitments which took her abroad. Were all the efforts of June and July to go for naught?

Mrs. Kelley determined to seize another opportunity of focusing public attention on radium poisoning. The annual meeting of the National Consumers League would be held in November, 1928, ending with a public dinner. To the dinner she assigned the grisly topic: *The Skeleton in Industry's Closet.* "A very beautiful kind of a skeleton," grimly commented Dr. Charles Norris, one of the principal speakers, "for the simple reason that by its own rays it has illuminated a very important subject."

If Mrs. Kelley planned to shock her audience and the public into renewed attention, she could not have contrived better.

Dr. Norris' speech was scientifically detached—and overwhelming. He had brought and passed around, as though in the laboratory, photographic films of the bones and the ash from various organs of a body which had been exhumed, four and a half years after burial, and which, as he explained, "had photographed themselves on account of their radium illumination." He reviewed briefly the history we have been following. "It was left to Dr. Martland to absolutely discover," as he put it, that the deaths of the dial painters were due to radium or mesothorium, "the evidence being similar to those that I have tried to show you in the films that I have passed around."

A momentary silence followed this speech before the audience recovered enough to applaud. Mrs. Franklin D.

Roosevelt, the toastmistress, spoke for us all in hailing a "far-reaching scientific study of industry in its very terrifying aspects."

Best of all, from the surgeon general came the long awaited assurance of the desired conference. It would be called, announced Dr. James P. Leake of the Public Health Service, in the near future. His words justified, if it needed justification, all Mrs. Kelley had done or could do in arousing widespread public concern over radium poisoning. "By focusing public attention on some of these horrible examples," said Dr. Leake, "the broader problems of disease prevention . . . can be greatly reduced. It was so in the tetra-ethyl lead work." He closed on an emotional but effective note, "The martyrdom of a few may save many."

The conference was held on December 20, 1928. Besides the doctors immediately concerned in the controversy, experts on radium were invited from the Bureau of Standards and the National Research Council, as well as representatives from state labor departments, the U. S. Public Health Service, the U. S. Bureau of Labor Statistics, and from various companies making radiolite equipment.

The conference passed a unanimous resolution asking the surgeon general to appoint two committees along lines suggested by Dr. Hamilton: first, a field investigation to study the conditions existing; and second, a committee to codify the best known methods of protection.

The next year, through the efforts of the state Consumers League, a bill was passed by the New Jersey Legislature adding radium necrosis to the list of compensable diseases under the Workmen's Compensation Act. New York in 1930 added to its list of compensable diseases radium poisoning from any process involving the use of radium or radioactive substance. (Previously the law had covered use of radium in hospitals only.)

A thorough investigation of dial-painting factories was made by the U. S. Public Health Service, with the committee of experts appointed after the conference acting in an advisory capacity. It was found that putting an end to the "pointing" of paint brushes with the lips had not solved the problem, since inhalation was a factor as well as ingestion. Drastic revision of all existing practices was held mandatory.[13]

Thus, the hazards of another lethal industrial poison were overcome, and the democratic process of government by informed public opinion was again justified. But the democratic process rests on continuous alertness. Twenty years later, in the summer of 1947, the death of some workers in plants using beryllium in the manufacture of fluorescent lights again raised the specter of an unknown industrial poison. History repeats itself. The plants, again, were in New Jersey. Dr. Martland, again, made the positive diagnosis. But the times had advanced so far that Dr. Martland's diagnosis, after some controversy, was accepted by his colleagues. Industrial medicine is now a recognized and well-established branch of the medical profession. The Consumers League of New Jersey took the lead in working for inclusion of beryllium poisoning among compensable industrial diseases—a better record than in radium poisoning but how far, still, from Florence Kelley's goal of studying industrial poisons "in advance, rather than through the death or disablement of the victims."

[13] Rigid and continuous inspection was recommended. To avoid accumulation of radioactive material in the workroom, mixed paint was to be given out to the workers in quantities to last preferably not longer than one hour. Painting by hand was to be done beneath a sheet of plate glass large enough to cover all the radioactive material, so that the face of the worker was not less than fourteen inches from the work. Adequate washing facilities, strict cleanliness of person and of premises, and routine medical examinations were to be provided and enforced.

Chapter 17

Florence Kelley in Retrospect

Florence Kelley died in 1932, in her seventy-fourth year. Now, with the perspective of twenty years, how important does her life and work appear? Today the things she worked for—government regulation of child labor, and of wages and hours, and government infant and maternity and other child care programs—all these are taken for granted (though, of course, efforts to raise standards in these fields continue). Probably many of the younger generation who are concerned with such laws assume that little had been achieved until the depression and Roosevelt's leadership brought about the federal legislation of the thirties. The pioneering state-by-state advance of the first quarter of the century and the first attempts to secure federal action are now history and tend to be forgotten. Florence Kelley's name, a symbol of the long fight for those early laws, is unknown to many who work in present-day campaigns to raise the federal minimum wage or strengthen the child labor provisions of the Fair Labor Standards Act. The truth is that New Deal Labor legislation did not spring full-blown. Its roots lie in the preceding thirty years or more, when our fast-developing industrialism led to state-by-state action to curb some of its worst abuses in the exploitation of labor.

Who demanded and secured these early state labor laws

in the face of the prevailing *laissez faire* philosophy of the period? It would be natural to assume that the demand came from organized labor, and in fact working men organized in labor unions did demand and secure certain laws for their own protection. But Mrs. Kelley's story is significant because it refutes that assumption, so far as a large and important area of labor legislation for women and children is concerned. The demand for laws to protect working women and children—for child labor, maximum hour, and minimum wage laws—came not from organized labor but from middle-class groups. The drive behind this demand was not self-interest but social conscience. And when the historian tries to piece together the detailed story of how those laws actually got passed in one state after another, he may well find himself adopting the "great man theory of history"—except that in this instance it was a great woman instead. Florence Kelley played a key role, and under her leadership a handful of individuals with no ax to grind produced phenomenal results. Their achievements look miraculous in the light of the expensive, highly organized campaigns needed nowadays to push a law through Congress or even through a state legislature.

Looking back at the end of twenty-five years of Consumers League activity, Mrs. Kelley herself recognized that progress in her chosen field was easier in the early years—probably because the opposition had not yet become well organized. "That was before the National Manufacturers' Association and the National Industrial Conference Board and many other great national organizations for slowing the national pace had got their stride," she said at the League anniversary meeting in 1925. "Everything we undertook was far easier and more glowingly hopeful than it is now."

But it was an immense job nonetheless that the tiny Consumers League undertook, involving, as Mrs. Kelley phrased it, "a great deal of effort to persuade legislatures, governors, presidents, and, most difficult of all, the courts."

And the woman who led this small dauntless band and gave it power far beyond its size? How did she do it? The secret of leadership is elusive. Some ingredients her fellow workers discerned:

"She made her generation think," was Lillian Wald's testimony to Florence Kelley's intellectual leadership.

"Thank you for believing that I shall accomplish something," Frances Perkins wrote her (on taking office as industrial commissioner of New York in 1929). "Your demand for good work and results has always been an inspiration, quite as much of an inspiration, I think, as your continued stream of new ideas."

Men as well as women responded to her intellectual leadership. John Graham Brooks, Newton D. Baker, John R. Commons, John H. Lathrop—four presidents of the Consumers League—testified to this fact, as well as men in other associations who counted on her "stream of ideas."

Newton Baker, himself a brilliant lawyer, wrote in 1937 (when attacks on Mrs. Kelley were revived in the fight against ratification of the child labor amendment), "My acquaintance with Florence Kelley for forty years was intimate and close. . . . From that acquaintance and from a rather constant and wide association with great women in America during my generation, I do not have any hesitation in saying that Mrs. Kelley was intellectually the greatest woman I have known."

W. E. B. DuBois spoke of the immense stimulus of her new ideas. "I have seen a dead Board galvanized, sometimes quite unwillingly, by her new queries, new orientation of thought, until we had convinced Mrs. Kelley that our conclusions were right, or just as often until she had convinced us that we were not ready for conclusions at all," he wrote of her participation in work for the rights of Negroes.

Florence Kelley's ideas were not only new, they were seminal. Her early recognition of the crucial role of judge-made laws was to be a liberal rallying ground of the twentieth century. Her early thoughts on labor administration were, in John R. Commons' words, "a revelation of what a labor department could be or do." Today her basic ideas on the rights of childhood and of working women have come to be generally accepted.

But there was something even more important than her ideas. George Alger, a New York lawyer who worked closely with her for years in many good causes, puts it thus: "Florence Kelley was one of the greatest and most successful pioneers in the long warfare against the bloodless and inhuman *laissez faire* economics. Into this warfare Florence Kelley put everything she had. She was a passionate soldier, a great advocate with a beautiful clear speaking voice and an extraordinary capacity for imparting moral earnestness in everything she said. She was tireless, a tremendous driving force for good." [1]

Everyone who associated with her felt the power of her personality with its central core of dauntless courage. All her life those who worked with her even briefly or infrequently were strengthened and refortified by their contact with her fearlessness. "Florence Kelley, who came into residence at Hull House in the winter of 1891, galvanized us all," wrote Jane Addams of the early years. "Everybody was brave from the moment she came into a room," wrote Newton Baker of her influence upon the War Department's labor policies in the First World War. "She was not afraid of truth, she was not afraid of life, she was not afraid of death, she was not afraid of enemies," said Lillian Wald at a memorial meeting. Added to her courage was an unbounded persistence. She never despaired, she would never admit that the fight was lost. As Frances Perkins put it, "She knew no discouragement and no despair, and when the rest of us were willing to give up . . . it was to her but the signal to begin again."

Florence Kelley's fighting spirit was surprisingly com-

---

[1] A personal, reminiscent letter.

bined with a predilection for the non-violent Quaker approach absorbed in her childhood in the home of her Quaker grandparents. This explained the patient perseverance of an otherwise naturally impatient person. No doubt it also explained her adherence to the pacifist position throughout the First World War. That pacifist conviction in turn caused her to throw herself with all the greater fervor into efforts to preserve labor standards despite wartime pressures.

Her belief in the Quaker approach to life led her in 1927 to join formally the Society of Friends. In the summers she would invite Friends to meet with her on Sundays at her Maine home at Naskeag. A friend describes how Mrs. Kelley started these Quaker meetings:

> Mrs. Kelley had seen a notice in the *Friends Intelligencer* directing chance Friends to a Meeting at the home of a solitary member of the Society wintering in Florida. At once she determined to do likewise. "Do you think anyone would come?" she asked eagerly. There could scarcely have been found a more unlikely place for traveling Friends than her cottage on isolated Naskeag. . . .
>
> That only a handful, already devoted to her, responded disheartened her not at all. "Despise not the day of small things," had been her watchword with which she comforted Consumers Leaguers, apologetic because an audience failed to materialize in the expected numbers. Enough for her that a half-dozen came to sit with her each Sunday afternoon, to share her glorious view and lift their hearts in the light of the sunset and of her dauntless spirit, or to sit by her fireside when storm or fog drove us inside.[2]

Perhaps it was the aspect of her nature which drew her to the Quaker faith which made Jane Addams her closest friend. She prized in Jane Addams a serene wisdom rooted in a more secure acceptance of the whole of life than she herself could ever achieve. Florence Kelley could never have been called serene. Newton Baker refers to her "fierce fidelity to the things that are true and beautiful." Probably

---

[2] *Friends Intelligencer,* Tenth Month, 1943, p. 6.

the circumstances of her life heightened the natural intensity of her nature. They strengthened her tendency to see life and people in black and white, to love and hate with an almost equal ardor. They reinforced her tendency to dramatize—source of strength and of weakness. The inner conflict in her nature was never wholly resolved.

Among the eminent women of her generation—her close friends—Lillian Wald had a more radiant personal charm; Julia Lathrop had greater sagacity in the ways of human behavior, partly intuitive, partly the fruit of her shrewdly pondered experience; Jane Addams had greater wisdom. But Florence Kelley above them all possessed a constantly flowing, inexhaustible life force, from which all could gain renewed strength. She was a woman on the heroic scale, generous and reckless of herself, with a genius for kindling others to serve—not herself, but the causes for which she made her plea, a plea impassioned yet always fortified by facts. Remarkable as were her achievements, Mrs. Kelley still lives, for all of us who knew her, more by what she was than by what she did. There was something about her infinitely greater than any of her deeds. Though for forty years she subordinated her personal life to her public work, we remember her as an individual, unique, colorful, contradictory, at once tender and capable of harshness, aggressive yet infinitely compassionate.

Index